Clyde Smith
Shanghai, China.
Jan. 1923

# THE
# POPULAR THEATRE

# *The*
# POPULAR THEATRE

*by*

## George Jean Nathan

*New York*
**ALFRED A. KNOPF**
*MCMXVIII*

PRINTED IN THE UNITED STATES OF AMERICA

" I deal not with theories, but with things as they are."— JOANNES CANTAC-UZENE.

# *Preface*

Mr. Ernest Newman, brought by vocational ordinances to review the sawings and mewlings of the heterogeneous catgut scrapers and contraband philomels who every other night were posturing themselves before London audiences as musicians and singers, became one day so riled at the whole business that he publicly announced he would no longer attend any performances save those of artists who had made a reputation. After fourteen years of unremitting theatre attendance in New York — a period during which I have nightly been spectator at the performances of authors, actors and managers who have made reputations — I am of a mind to announce that I will no longer attend any performances save those of authors, actors and managers who have not made a reputation.

To the making of a reputation in the popular theatre of New York, everything would seem to be essential but talent. One is so surrounded in this theatre by famous playwrights, famous actors and famous producers — all more or less first-rate eighth-rate men — that the occasional glimpse of an utterly unknown, utterly unidentified, intruder bursts upon the vision with a sensation as agreeable æsthetically as the sudden spectacle, on a dark, gloomy, rainy day in Spring, of a young woman in a soft white dress with a pink flower on her hat. It is in no small degree to such newcomers that the critic of the theatre looks for stimulation and cheer. For years the critic has watched with leaden eye and numbed brain-pan the uninspired antics of so endless a noctambulation of celebrated authorlets and anointed dudelers that his hope is ever for the new unknown, for the writer who has never composed a play that has run five hundred nights on Broadway, for the actor whose name has never contributed to a theatre program the appearance of the first page of the *Evening Journal,* for the producer who has never been compared in the ebullient newspapers to Reinhardt or Stanislawsky or Adolph Appia. He waits patiently through a dozen plays by famous dramatists of Broadway for a play by some unknown Edward Massey, through a dozen performances by famous actors of Broadway for the performance of some unknown Opal Cooper, through a dozen productions by famous producers of Broadway for a production like that of " The Poor Fool " by some unknown amateur out of Washington Square. The fame of the American popular theatre gives us dramas by Jane Cowl and Otto Hauerbach, acting like that of Robert Edeson and Holbrook Blinn, productions like those of " Upstairs and Down " and " Daybreak." The obscurity of the American popular theatre gives us plays by Eugene O'Neill, acting like that of the highly adroit amateur at the Neighbourhood Playhouse, productions like those of the beginner Hopkins' " Poor Little Rich Girl " and the beginner Williams' " Justice " and the beginner Kugel's " Old Lady 31."

[ 8 ]

# PREFACE

In any one season in the popular theatre of New York, it is doubtful if there are presented out of the two hundred or so annual productions, more than five or six at most that are prosperous in the amusement of a man tutored to a point of skepticism that hiccoughs may be stopped by counting slowly up to one hundred. For the major part, the plays presented are melodramas exhibiting the news that a man's better nature plus a church-organ will inevitably triumph over his impulse to short-change the cash register; librettos discovering the Atellan juices in the conceit that married Frenchmen always sneak away from their wives on the night of the Quat'-z-Arts ball and that the wives, accompanied by their maids, invariably track after them and make them jealous by flirting with Raoul, the huzzar; and problem dramas demonstrating that every time a married woman is on the point of embarking on the *Maurentic* with her lover she is at the last moment dissuaded from her purpose by the falling ill of her baby boy. Nowhere, not even in the Metropolitan Museum of Art, may one encounter so scintillating an array of mediocrity promulgated in so pretentious a manner. But — "Have success," wrote Edouard Pailleron, "and there shall always be fools to say that you have talent." And so it has come about that the theatre, as we of the American today know it, is a great savanna of successful business men who are mistaken for and hailed as talented producers and successful showmakers and facemakers who are mistaken for and hailed respectively as talented dramatists and actors.

This condition of affairs is, of course, quickly

traceable to the radiant gullibility of us Americans, in the theatre probably as nowhere else. No worm-medicine vendor, exhorting the cross-road yokel with his charmed philtre, had ever so simple a constitu-ency. Let some Macdonald Hastings come along with direct transcripts from the speculations of Rochefoucauld which he places into play form and calls "The New Sin" and by the next sunrise the almanacs are rich in praise of a famous new philoso-pher-dramatist. Let some A. E. Thomas appear with an unacknowledged counterpart of the French play, "Son Père," which he announces as a new and original comedy called "The Rainbow," and for months afterward we hear paternosters to the famous new American comedy writer. Let some clever showman like the Frederic Thompson that was, a man who in his day understood well this native gulli-bility and shrewdly catered to it, have his press-agent announce that he was so deep a believer in verisimili-tude that he actually maneuvered the bunch-lights in the wings in such wise that the scenic trees would cast changing shadows as in the actual sunlight, and from the one end of the boulevard to the other spreads the awe. And once the Broadway species of fame, the popular species of reputation, fastens itself upon a person of the theatre, it clings like a leech to him, self-confirmed and irremovable. The foundation for this fame, this reputation, matters not. It may be intrinsically little more than a curl, as in the case of some Della Fox; or little more than a rumour that the peculiar coiffure is designed to hide missing ears, as in the case of some Cléo de Mérode; or little

[10]

more than a pair of aphrodisiac eyes or pink pajamas or sightly limbs. Yet fame proceeds from the wake of each, a fame that overshadows mere genuine talent, mere authentic skill.

Thus, the fame of Mary Anderson sprang less from her considerable ability as an actress than from her reputation for being a virtuous woman; the fame of Mrs. James Brown Potter less from her talent than from her spectacular matrimonial alliance with an affluent and tony New Yorker; the fame of Richard Mansfield less from his fine performances upon the stage than from his private Pullman and the tales of his temperamental didoes in the wings; and the fame of William Gillette less from his unmistakable dexterity in the fashioning of adroit farce and melodrama than from the report that he had consumption and took long walks at two A. M. in the solitude of Central Park. And what was true yesterday is even more true today. Idiosyncrasy and talent are as often confounded as monetary success and talent. Hang the stage with strips of tar-paper and hang the strips of tar-paper with small slices of Salami and you are hailed a great innovator in the matter of scenic embellishment. Illuminate brightly with numerous baby spotlights the faces of the actors in a scene calling for a pitch dark dungeon and you are celebrated as a master producer. Take a trifle longer over your make-up box and cuckoo the performance of Irving in "Waterloo" and you are chaired as a magnificent actor.

But, slowly, the young idea is creeping into the theatre. And, slowly, the old frauds, and the way

[11]

of estimating them, are being backed out of the stage door. Not that youth, and the changes that youth inevitably brings with it, are automatically ever for the better. But this youth that is coming into the American playhouse has about it a pleasant air, and one that augurs well. It is slowly giving us new dramatists of ability in the place of the famous charlatans we have come to know; it is gradually giving us new producers of skill and vision and education in the place of the celebrated Philistines. And it is quite possible that in time — it may be ten years, it may be twenty — it will give us also, out of its better labours, a new and a finer audience in the place of the present herd of hallelujahing song-writers, motion picture actors and Broadway bounders whose illiterate voice is the voice of the illiterate audience whose voice in turn is the illiterate voice of our native popular theatre.

# *Contents*

# The
# Popular Theatre

# Chapter One: The Popular Theatre

To an appreciable extent, the persistent poverty of our national stage may be said to be due to the dissemination and promiscuous swallowing of the second-hand theory of such well-meaning but naïve old gentlemen as the Messrs. Brander Matthews, Richard Burton and troupe, the theory, to wit, that the theatre is essentially a democratic institution and must so remain or perish from the earth. Imposing structures of conscientious piffle have been reared upon this foundation. The gospel has been hung around the neck of the college boy, disembogued in the lecture chamber, cuckooed by the Drama Leaguers. And yet, at bottom, one finds it as absurd and inutile as the paragrandine or the New York State Adultery Act. Not absurd and inutile, true enough, when trajected and practised by the frank hawker of theatrical asafœtida, but worse than absurd and inutile when exhibited by the critic or commentator professing a cultural standard somewhat above that obtaining in a young girls' finishing school or Columbia University.

From any plane of æsthetic criticism higher than that from which one appraises the literature of Mrs. E. Burke Collins, the art of Austin O. Spare and Frederick Carter, the music of Charles K. Harris,

the drama of R. C. Carton — or the dramatic
criticism of such Drama League bell-wethers — the
theatre is to be necessarily regarded as an institution of an essential aristocracy: an aristocracy of
beautiful letters, of ideas and wit, of viewpoint and
philosophy. To hold the contrary, to hold the
theatre a mere recess pasture for the potwallopers,
a suave dive for the proletarian taste on the loose,
is to make shift to establish and appraise an art in
terms of the number of its admirers — to place a
lithograph of Mr. Fatty Arbuckle above Rembrandt's portrait of Turenne, "The Very Idea"
above Rittner's "En Route," or the autopsies of
Rabindranath Tagore above those of Rammohun-
Roy. If it be true that the theatre is intrinsically
a popular institution, a saloon for the locofocos,
then it is equally true — and clearly — that the
dramatic criticism concerned with this institution
must amount to little more than a rebabbling of
the mob esteems and projection and coronation of
the mob criteria. And, being from this point of
view true, one doubtless discovers here an account-
ing for the emptiness and banality of such dramatic
criticism as the *curriculacocci* periodically unload
upon the public prints.

From that side of the theatre which has been
regarded as democratic, there has come down to us
most of the rant and jabber, most of the pish and
platitude, that in very slightly disguised form contrives still to overawe and enchant the pleasure-
seeking skipjack and confound any man who has
arrived at a sufficient altitude of scholarship to be

[18]

able to differentiate between Meyerbeer and Schlitz's. From that side has come the stuff of such as D'Ennery and Cormon, Bulwer-Lytton, Sardou, John M. Morton, Mrs. Henry Wood, Dumas *fils*, Boucicault — the " Two Orphans," the " Toscas," the " East Lynnes," the " Camilles " and the " Boxes and Coxes." From the side of aristocracy, from the theatre designed originally for the few, have come the Molières, whose Palais-Royal company was authorized " the troupe of the King," the Shakespeares, who came under the patronage of the circles of King James and Elizabeth, the Ibsens, who had to look to an artist of the violin for their first practical theatrical encouragement and who " had to make their way against the dullest and most disheartening of mob influences," the Hauptmanns, who were given to the theatre in the cradle of the anti-herd Freie Bühne of Otto Brahm and Paul Schlenther, and on down the list to the Bernard Shaws of the moment who, for their first hearings, have had to rely on private societies and closed doors. The democratic theatres have been the theatres of Sir Augustus Harris and Daniel Frohman; the aristocratic theatres those of Stanislawsky and Dantschenko, André Antoine and Lugné Poë, Max Halbe and Josef Rüderer. The democratic theatre of our more recent America has given us, as among its most popular examples, " Way Down East," " The Old Homestead " and " Experience." This same democratic theatre has given us, as among its most summary failures, the plays of Molnar, Brieux, Hauptmann, Galsworthy, Brighouse, Donnay, Hervieu, Capus, Bahr, Chesterton. . . .

Statistics are the refuge of the unimaginative. I shall refrain from physicking you with the one hundred and one chronicles that, like a witch's wand out of Grimm, transform the professor-critics into so many *asclepiadaceæ*. I shall omit a recording of such statistics as concern the Moscow Artistic Theatre, that amazingly successful and tonic institution which was based on the theory of exclusiveness and insured that exclusiveness by being among other things the most expensive of Russian playhouses, its admission fees surpassing the charges even of the Imperial Theatres. Or of such statistics as relate to the so-called undemocratic private theatres of the Enemy Nation, happy enterprises that have borne the torch of a finer and better drama into the Teutonic conscience and the consciences of further-flung countries — the theatres of such as Reinhardt, Grube, Dumont and Lindemann. Every one save the professor-critics must already be privy to such dry news of the yesterdays. . . . The critic who in this day views the theatre as a popular institution is the critic who views the novel as a popular institution, and so holds Miss Leona Dalrymple a more accomplished and accomplishing craftsman than Anatole France, Enrico Butti or Joseph Conrad. . . . Art is ever a butler in Childs'.

But there is small call for the professorial *cameriere* to worry. Our theatre remains perfectly safe for the mob. For one evening with Shaw at even his worst (" Misalliance "), one evening the

[20]

humour of which is at least derived from characters falling upon one another's ideas instead of upon their own plump-places, there is still a luxuriance of procursive epilepsies in which imprisoned emotional actresses bang and bawl vainly for help against locked doors, with a telephone in plain sight not two feet away (" Branded "), and in which (" Lombardi, Ltd.") a hot-blooded Italian magnificently declines to kiss his beloved until she is duly married to him.

In a popular theatre, the best in drama and dramatic literature must inevitably fail. In a popular, or mob, theatre, there can prosper no satire, for satire presupposes a blasé mind and attitude, whereas the mob mind and attitude are ever the mind and attitude of a child looking into a shop window at Christmastime, dismayed at the wonders of paint and tinsel. Satire inverts the popular opinion and pours the sawdust out of that opinion. To the popular opinion, therefore, satire is, clearly enough, incomprehensible, unintelligible. The popular play is that play which pours the sawdust not out, but *in;* the play that enthrones ignorance, flatters unfounded vanity; the play, in short, that stuffs the greatest amount of excelsior into the wax doll. So, too, straightforward psychology must fail, straightforward transcription of moods, feelings and reactions, for, save in the more primitive forms of melodrama and farcical comedy, the mob is stranger to the characters of authentic drama and anæsthetic to their impulses, thoughts and deportment. In a country like our own, where the average man thinks himself a devil when the manicurist, on finishing her chore, gives him a familiar little tap on the hand, it is unlikely that a brilliant searching into the pathology of amour, such, for example, as is instanced in that excellent scene in Act II of " Over the 'Phone," will meet with appreciation or understanding. Schnitzler is not for the man in whose veins flows the hot tzigane blood of Pottstown, Pa. De Curel is not for the woman the supreme passion of whose life has consisted in an ocular *liaison* with the celluloid ghost of Mr. Francis X. Bushman, nor John Galsworthy for the otherwise good citizen whose idea of dramatic literature is anything with a pistol in it.

The popular theatre, the world over, is a theatre whose constituents are interested solely in such dramatic pieces as reflect their own thoughts and emotions, as repeat to their ears those things they already know and feel. To determine the quality of the popular theatre, therefore, it is but necessary to catalogue the qualities of the audience of that theatre. What, for example, does the average native theatre audience believe? Not the above-the-average audience one encounters periodically when a play of merit dawns upon the community, but the audience one sees nightly in the average show-shop of commerce? In the first place, the sum total of its book knowledge — I think I am not too unfair — is probably that of the public high-school pupil in his second scholastic year. In the second place, the sum total of its worldly knowledge is probably that of the average moderately well-to-do suburban shopkeeper. In the third place, the sum total of its emotional and æsthetic adventure may be approached in terms of a composite of professional baseball game, phonograph, street-car flirtation and California claret. In the fourth place, the sum total of its common faith may be indicated, impressionistically, in its belief that the farmer is an honest man and greatly imposed upon; that morality consists in the repeal of physiology by law; that a sudden chill is a sign that somebody is walking over one's grave; that some ignoble Italian is at the bottom of every Dorothy Arnold *fugax;* that all male negroes can sing; that a tarantula will not crawl over a piece of rope; that millionaires always go to sleep at the opera; that Paderewski can get all the pianos he wants for nothing; that Gavarni was a composer and Debureau a painter; that minestra is the name of a particular kind of Italian soup; that Henry James never wrote a short sentence; and that all dachshunds come from Germany.

The theatrical stimuli to which this audience gives emotional response are correlatively ingenuous. Any scene, however badly written, in which an actor comes out on the stage carrying a dog that is supposed to have been run over by a motor-car driven by the villain, will set the audience to polyphonous sniffling and to an almost audible vituperation of the heinous chauffeur. And any scene, however crude, that exhibits an inebriated gentleman in the act of disrobing for bed without removing his top hat, will with equal certainty brew a series of amazing guffaws. It is needless to elaborate on this theme: if you search for further examples, I refer you to one of the best treatises on the subject that has ever come to my attention, a treatise which appears in a volume of admirable critical papers entitled " Another Book on the Theatre." But the facts are plain, and unmistakable. A first-rate play is four times in five doomed by these tokens to failure in the mob theatre.

I speak here not alone of our American mob theatre. The outstanding mob theatre, in almost any country one elects, is comparatively the theatre of parageusia, the barrack of balderdash, the cow-house of art. The mob theatre of London disgorges " The Man Who Stayed at Home " and " Mr. Wu " and " Bella Donna." The esoteric theatre of London, typified by such institutions as the Incorporated Stage Society and the Play Actors, gives us " Change " and " Points of View," " Chains " and " The Polygon "— the plays of men like Shaw and Francis, Moore and Yeats, Brighouse and Bennett, in the place of plays by such Strand Ibsens as Cecil Raleigh and Bernard Fagan. The mob theatre of Paris gives us " Samson," " La Rampe " and " La Flambée "; the aristocratic theatre, " Barbarine " and Bruneau's " Faute de l'Abbé Mouret " out of Zola, and " L'Eau de Vie." The mob theatre of Berlin unloads such so-called crook and bull plays as " Piquebube " and " Excellenz Max "; the theatre of the elect provides Hauptmann and Wedekind and Ludwig Thoma. In the mob theatre of Vienna we find such militant, obstreperous twaddle as August Riemer's " Austria

[24]

Has All the Virtues "; in the aristocratic theatre, Felix Salten. I allude in these latter instances, clearly enough, to what is confessedly the mob theatre, for in all countries save the Anglo-Saxon — whether in Russia or France or Italy or in the enemy lands — the essentially popular theatre is overshadowed by the theatre of suavity and distinction. Yet the mob theatre, wherever you find it and when find it you do, is the theatre of lost ideals. . . . Laugh how you will at the lamented New Theatre of New York, but the truth about that theatre is that, during the period of its initial isolations and snobberies, it produced more good plays than were ever produced during a like period in the history of any other American playhouse.

\* \* \*

Among plays that tend to make the local theatre unsafe for the multitude one finds occasionally such a manuscript as the " Misalliance " of Shaw. Between the acts of this play, my colleague, Mr. Clayton Hamilton, proclaimed to me that if ever he wrote a play so deficient in the matter of structural technique, he hoped I would shoot him. Now, I am fond of Hamilton, and I am not disposed to shoot him until his turn comes (there are something like five colleagues on the waiting list ahead of him), but I am always willing to oblige a friend. Especially when he so mistakes a remarkable proficiency in structural technique for a deficiency. The truth about Shaw, of course, is that he understands the accepted structural technique so well that he is able to discard it. The best business man in the theatre today (I refer you to his illuminating correspondence with Harold Brighouse), he appreciates that what makes money in the theatre is novelty, and that since the accepted play-writing technique lacks novelty, the best way to make money is to reject that technique and substitute for it a technique that is unusual and unconventional. Shaw has made, to date, two hundred and twenty thousand dollars out of the theatre. His royalties are fifteen per cent., flat, of the gross — and they have come to him at this rate from America, England, Germany, France, Austria and Russia. And, while making this money, he has at the same time made a striking reputation for himself as the wittiest, freshest and the most unusual dramatic author of his time. And how has he done these things? He has done them, very simply, by doing what no one else has been doing. To believe that Shaw, who has been writing for the theatre for twenty years, who is a man of education and vision, and who is the leading dramatist of the Anglo-Saxon theatre — to believe that this man has tried vainly to master the sort of structural technique that such a Piccadilly bunk-butcher as Horace Annesley Vachell contrived easily to master at the first crack, is indeed a job for the super-yogi.

It is claimed by some that did Shaw understand the technique which he currently foregoes, his plays would be better plays. In other words, that if he wrote his plays in accordance with the ritual of Sardou or Emile Augier, those plays would be greatly improved. To me, at least, this seems much

[26]

like arguing that Richard Strauss' songs for baritone and orchestra would be much better if the composer had written them after the formulæ of Verdi, or that Paul Cézanne were a more agreeable painter did he emulate the feminine perfumeries of Henner. That Shaw understands perfectly the technique of the theatre is evident to anyone who cares to go to the trouble of studying closely his plays, and their effect upon a theatrical audience. If ever there lived a so-called sure-fire dramatist, Shaw is that man. (*Ref. Lecture III, Augustin Hamon, Faculté des Lettres de l'Université de Paris.*) " Your technique," Hamon has written to Shaw, " is that of the great comic writers of the ancient Greeks and Latins of the Middle Ages, of the Elizabethan period, of Molière, of Le Sage and of Beaumarchais. And your technique is that of these latter by reason of your comic wit. And in the future, no one will be able to write a high comedy of ideas and of characters without using this technique which is inherent and necessary to this form of comedy." But more than this, Shaw has brought to this technique an executive showmanship doubtless hitherto unmatched in the instance of a first-rate man of the theatre. He is at once an artist and an excellent business man, a mixture of Royal Academician and Gimbel Brothers.

That Shaw understands thoroughly the sure-fire of the theatre, the most positively provocative devices, and that he adroitly employs these devices on the numerous occasions when the dollar-grabber in him gets the better of the artist, should be manifest to anyone who has observed even a small part of his work. When he makes Dudgeon strut like a hero, the laugh is as sure-fire as when Richard Harding Davis makes Willie Collier strut like a hero in the last act of "The Dictator." The drunk Patiomkin in "Great Catharine" is as sure-fire a laugh-getter as the drunk Leon Errol in "Hitchy-Koo"; the allusion to the portly Mrs. Warren as a sparrow as sure as the allusion to the chambermaid in "Mary's Ankle" as a cheese; the sudden propulsion of Edstaston upon his rearo as sure as the similar business disclosed upon the stage of the Columbia Theatre. He is privy to the guffaw-sesame of the cuss word; of the repeated mispronunciation of a character's name, as with the Szczepanowska in "Misalliance," a sure-fire device that was one of the Hoyt standbys and is currently relied upon by such comiques as Raymond Hitchcock and George Munroe; of word reiteration, as in "Candida," after the manner of Sam Bernard's "Sufficiency"; of the irrelevant employment of precise language in a slang situation, as in the case of a De Wolf Hopper curtain speech; of the mimicry of one character by another, as in "You Never Can Tell," a trick being used currently at the end of the first act of "Business Before Pleasure," and gaining the loudest laugh of the season. He is privy, too, to the irresistible tear that lurks ever in the scene of leavetaking (as in "Cæsar and Cleopatra"), and in the scene of sympathetic rejection of an ill-favoured suitor (as in "Candida"). And he knows, as well, the sure-fire trick of smashing glass ("Misalliance "), the trick of melodramatic bugle-calls and stabbings and general hullaballoo (" Cæsar and Cleopatra "), the trick of suave smut (there is a startling example in " Misalliance "), the trick of sensational smut (" Mrs. Warren "), and the trick of bringing on the marines of the U. S. S. *Santiago* to rescue the hero in the grand finale (" Brassbound ").

Imagine a man like this, a man admitted to be one of the two greatest living dramatists, a man whose plays have been done in every civilized country under the sun, a man whose vision is the best in all England, a man whose influence has been felt in every theatre save the theatre of Spain and Italy — imagine such a man, *mon très cher* Hamilton, being unable to write, if write he would, the technically exact sort of plays written by Mr. Willard Mack!

# Chapter Two: Its Plays

That the popular play is by sound standards ninety-nine times in one hundred a bad play is a scandal long since interred in the P's under Platitude. But, save for the occasional vague theorizing of the theatrical anchorites who pass for authorities on the drama in the one-building universities, the reasons for the automatic badness of the popular play are rarely inquired into. And when these reasons are inquired into, they are invariably either jocosely diverted with some such observation as that the popular play must reflect the intellectual sophistication of a public forty-nine out of fifty of whose individuals believe that a cinder may be removed from one eye by massaging the other, or suffocated with some such collegiate pastille as " Even the most cultured and intellectual of men when he forms an atom of a crowd loses consciousness of his acquired mental qualities and harks back to his primal nakedness of mind; the dramatist, therefore, because he writes for a crowd, writes for an uncivilized and uncultivated mind."

Each of these amiable attitudes and the characteristic and reminiscential train of reasoning it produces is alike false in that it is based upon the assumption that intellectuality and meritorious drama go hand

[30]

in hand and that the popular play must be a bad play since it is fashioned to appeal to a crowd mechanically or otherwise bereft of intellectuality. Nothing, of course, could be further from the truth. In the first place, there is generally no more intellectual content in the first-rate play than in the hack play designed for the mob. The basic philosophy of Ibsen's " The Master Builder " is indistinguishable from that of Madeline Lucette Ryley's " Mice and Men," precisely as the basic philosophy of Sudermann's " Happiness in a Corner " is indistinguishable from that of Fred Jackson's " The Naughty Wife." Cosmo Hamilton's yokel-yanker, " The Blindness of Virtue," is intrinsically of an intellectual piece with Wedekind's first-rate " Awakening of Spring," and Hemmerde and Neilson's rabble tickler, " The Butterfly on the Wheel," is of the same fundamental metaphysic as Björnson's " Geography and Love."

Again, such first-rate plays as Hauptmann's " The Weavers " and Galsworthy's " Strife," both prompt popular failures, are of so intellectually simple a nature that they are within the grasp of even the most feeble mob intelligence, whereas such specious, defective plays, and plays promptly popular, as Augustus Thomas' " Witching Hour " and Belasco's " Return of Peter Grimm " are built upon themes like mental suggestion and the domination of the subsconscious that assuredly would seem to be mob caviare. Brieux's " Les Hannetons," Pinero's " Thunderbolt," Echegaray's " El Gran Galeoto " and any number of other first-rate distinctly unpopular plays are intrinsically of a psychodynamic content not

[31]

nearly so difficult of agglomerate digestion as
Locke's " Case of Becky," Thomas' " As a Man
Thinks " and any number of other eighth-rate dis-
tinctly popular plays.

Still again, a first-rate play like Galsworthy's
" Justice," written by an artist with the mob far
from mind, becomes a popular play where a tenth-
rate play like Megrue's and Cobb's " Under Sentence," frankly written by Broadway for Broadway, and retailing the same theme as the Galsworthy work, becomes an unpopular play. Björnson's " The Gauntlet," listed by the professors as
an unpopular play because of its so-called intellectuality, remains still an unpopular play when this so-
called intellectuality is reduced to terms of Times
Square by Rachel Crothers in " A Man's World."
So, too, with Tolstoi's " Living Corpse " when made
into the more transpicuous Ditrichstein version of the
" Temperamental Journey," with Björnson's " Leon-
arda " when reduced to Kellett Chambers' " The
Right to Happiness," with Brieux's " La Foi " and
Moody's " The Faith Healer " when reduced to
George Cohan's " The Miracle Man," with Hervieu's " La Loi de l'Homme " and Geraldine Bon-
ner's " Sauce for the Goose," with Ibsen's " Pillars
of Society " and Hurlbut's " The Writing on the
Wall," with Hauptmann's " Lonely Lives " and Eugene Walters' " Just a Wife," with Strindberg's
" Father " and Paul Armstrong's " Bludgeon " . . .

Out of this topsy-turvy it would appear to be no
facile job to deduce the badness of the popular play
on grounds of absence or even subordinacy of intel-

lectuality. And so we turn for proof to the professorial theory that the popular play is a bad play since it is written for the mob, and since the mob lowers automatically the intelligence of its component individuals. Here, for all the sonorous eloquence of the university Dupins, we find ourselves afresh confounded. The Le Bon and Tarde notion, gobbled whole by the jerkwater Solomons, to the effect that the collective psychology of the crowd is instrumental in reducing the intelligence and poise of that crowd to the lowest common denominator is more often anything but true. While it may be true of a crowd in a gin-mill or circus sideshow, or of a crowd at a prize-fight or dinner party or dance, it is worse than imbecile to hold it true of a crowd in the theatre or in an art gallery or at a symphony concert. Take the lowest type of crowd imaginable, the type in which there is not more than one half-civilized man to every hundred, the crowd, for example, at a professional baseball game, and bundle that crowd bag and baggage into some great Carnegie Hall where they are playing Beethoven's Fifth. What would happen? At first, undoubtedly, a great deal of loud snickering and oh sassafras and bandying of sour *mots* and let's get the hell out o' this morgue. And what then? A slowly settling mass, a crowd gradually — very gradually perhaps — accommodating itself to its accursed surroundings, a crowd gradually shaming itself up to the conduct of its more genteel and more cultured and more disciplined component parts — and a crowd listening at length if, true enough, not entirely with interest and sympathy, at

[33]

least with open mind and in respectful silence.

Such a mob, instead of being lowered to its average indecorum and stupidity, as the professors maintain, is rather elevated in varying degree to its leaven of gentility and intelligence. The intelligent man in a mixed crowd retains at least the basic share of his intelligence and the yahoo in the same crowd becomes more or less uncomfortably inoculated with that man's intelligence. Take a first-rate play, like Shaw's " Cæsar and Cleopatra." Fill the house with twelve intelligent men and twelve hundred noodles. When the twelve hundred noodles boo, do the twelve intelligent men boo, or feel like booing? But when the twelve intelligent men applaud, is it not a fact that the twelve hundred noodles, even if they fail to join in or fail to feel like joining in, yet become inwardly just a trifle dubious as to their own apathy? And does not the applause of the lonely dozen put the twelve hundred noodles willynilly in a slightly more hospitable attitude toward the piece?

But here, I admit, I am guilty of giving the toe to one theory with what after all is merely another theory. So let us try facts. One will be sufficient. The notion of the professors that a theatrical crowd is, like a street-corner gathering, ever a mere casual crowd, and that it may so be used as a stable and unchanging specimen in psychological research, is based on the perfectly obvious delusion that the crowds that go to the forty-odd New York theatres of an evening are entirely different and distinct crowds on each succeeding evening of the season. The opposite is, of

[34]

course, true. The theatrical crowd of New York, and of any other city, big or small, is to a preponderant degree a fixed and sharply defined crowd, a crowd that has been going to the theatre for a variable number of years, a crowd gradually finding its tastes polished by its better element, and so presently being graduated from the slap-stick farce of " Charley's Aunt " to the satiric farce of de Caillavet's and de Flers' " The King," from the tin piano " Earl and the Girl " to the melodious " Merry Widow," from the stodgy slop of Charles Klein to the humour of Clare Kummer and the wit of Jesse Lynch Willians. The dramatist, therefore, because he writes for this crowd, does not necessarily write, as the professors imagine, for a fitfully heterogeneous auditorium mind, crude, untrained and refractory. Hence, since the writers of the popular plays do not, anyway, agree with the professors as to the mediocrity of the crowd's intellectual attainments, and since they conscientiously write the very best plays they know to write, the reason for the automatic badness of the popular play is not to be found here. Where then? Very simply, I daresay, in the automatic badness of the theatre itself. The theatre, that is, as potential bazaar of art.

To the devastating whims of the theatre the first-rate play and the tenth-rate play are equally subject; and if the former play suffers less and less often than the latter play it is simply because its creator happens by nature and instinct to be stubborn and independent artist where the creator of the bad play happens either constitutionally or by an acquired mental cheapness to be a conscious or unconscious seeker after mere clap and coin. But, as dramatists pure and simple, as workers for the stage, the Gerhart Hauptmanns and the Eugene Walters are handicapped by the same arbitrary theatrical shortcomings and idiosyncrasies which the illuminated platform imposes upon them. The theory that the Hauptmanns, unlike the Walters, write their plays with the acting stage far from mind is akin to the theory that Ibsen unintentionally revolutionized dramatic, which is to say stage, technique by intentionally writing his plays primarily for the library.

Against these crude impositions and impostures of the stage the artist fights more sturdily and sagaciously than the hack, and his play is hence most often a play not so unavoidably bad. Bad, that is, from the viewpoint of a sound and complete work of art: in comparison, for example, with a sound novel, a sound painting, or a sound piece of music. Where the novelist, the painter, or the composer faces one rule, the dramatist faces a dozen, eight of which are extrinsic to his art, and all of which are at best half-crazy. In order to achieve the essential theatrical unbroken leg-work on the part of his actors, Shakespeare had to stoop in his greatest tragedy to the baldest of bald stage artifices. Barrie, after he had finished " Peter Pan," had arbitrarily to tinker with the perfectly imagined scene of his well-planned and well-executed second act in order to make it stageworthy. For the one uncompromising Hauptmann of " Lonely Lives," there are the two stage compromising Hauptmanns of " Griselda " and " Elga."

Brieux writes " La Foi " to the full of his imagination and then is forced to pull in his reins with a malapropos jerk that the work may be made playable. Imagine cutting three-quarters of an hour out of the reading of Conrad's novel " Lord Jim," as they must out of the playing of Ibsen's " Wild Duck " to fit it into the stage scheme of things. Imagine a stage which inexorably makes Shaw chop out the best part of his " Man and Superman."

The artist, of course, fights tooth and nail against the stage's stupid ritual and though that ritual, for all his valour, generally gets him one way or another in the end, his crucified play remains yet a variably good play for the simple reason that, unlike the mere gack merchant, he has declined to surrender to the egregious ritual without something of a scrap. But, even so, the pugnacious spirit of the artist-dramatist very often presently dies, and he realizes the futility of the fight, and hoists a white flag marked but slightly, for personal respect's sake, with the purple of his art. Thus, a Pinero surrenders with a " Mind-the-Paint-Girl," a Galsworthy with a " Fugitive," a Brieux with a " Damaged Goods." . . .

The frankly popular playmaker, on the other hand, hoists the milk-white flag immediately he gets on his uniform and before he can see, even remotely, the whites of the enemy's eggs. He declines to take any chances whatever. He appreciates, and accurately, that the law of the theatre and its stage demands that he commit a thousand and one artistic incongruities and absurdities like emotionalizing a composition generically and properly unemotional,

[37]

like making active an essentially passive picture, and like inculcating the character of a drone with a quick, suspensive interest, and so he goes ahead and without further ado commits them. He has amiably learned his lesson, not out of his own experience, but out of the experiences of superior artists and craftsmen. He has seen that the difference between art and the drama is the difference between " Vanity Fair," the novel, on the one side, and " Vanity Fair," the dramatized novel, on the other — even where the dramatization is the work of a playmaker, himself an artist, like Langdon Mitchell . . . Conrad's " Youth " is a work of art. Is a playable play, treating of the same subject and treated even with the same great artistry, conceivable?

The popular play, therefore, is generally a bad play for the same reason that the music that emanates from a mouth-harmonica is bad music. The medium of expression, however good the intentions of the performer, is too primitive, too greatly curtailed, too insufficient. The drama, good or bad, is an art in handcuffs. And the degree in which it differs is merely the degree in which the wrists of its creator are limber. But, good or bad, it is an art bounded by the same cramping and grotesque frontiers, on this side by some such proscription as Aristotle's artistically ironic unities, on that by some such coop as the peremptory drop-curtain, on this again by objective action and on that again by over-emphasis of so-called " plot." That a Shakespeare has with high success flouted certain of these many baroque limbos and that a Chekhov has with moderate success flouted certain others is contention of a kidney with that which maintains a jail to be an institution designed for the escape of its inmates on the ground that once in a blue moon some virtuoso of the can-opener composes for himself an exit.

# Chapter Three: Its Broadway and Its Playwrights

The common gymnastic which has for its major gesture the blaming of Broadway, and what Broadway represents, for all that is worst in the American drama is grounded on a fallacy not less fantastic than the current educational philosophy which holds it practicable so to codify a youngster's instruction that he shall learn nothing save that which will be useful to him in his adult years. The bane of the American drama is not Broadway, but Fifth Avenue. Broadway, and the essence of Broadway, its spirit and æsthetic, have given to America what of peculiar individuality and freshness its native drama possesses, where Fifth Avenue — or at least the oblique influence of Fifth Avenue — has more often scuttled the ship.

The majority of our popular playwriters are, by nativity and upbringing, products of Broadway. This one, when at an age when other little boys were being roundly spanked for so much as venturing to ask their parents just what it was Hannah Elias was doing to make her famous, was already embellishing the vaudeville stage and swatting his father on the nose with a newspaper upon an exchange of *double entente* on the Princess Chimay. And that one, while at the age when most babies are still having their little Keystones tenderly sprinkled with talcum, was already being projected violently upon his from up out a trap-door in one of David Henderson's extravaganzas.

Of such, in considerable part, our American play-composers: grown-up stage children, ex-ushers, ex-callboys, ex-actors, ex-advance agents. And where not precisely of this gender, alumni — we find in *Who's Who* — of such pertinent literary and artistic callings as freight-train conductor, hotel clerk, carpenter, stock-broker, circus acrobat, shop-keeper and shoe salesman. Of training in the arts, of training in the graces of gentility and good breeding, of the cultural poise and outlook that come from careful preparation and careful education and association with the finished and adventured peoples of the world, from first to last scarcely a trace, scarcely a clue. Rather a sure swagger, a knock-'em-out-of-their-seats sort of artistry, a brash but not unfacile command of the elementary hokums of the theatre, a loud and brazen, yet clever, trading in the biff-bang melodramatics and slam-bang farce stuffs — but no reserve, no deliberation, no whimsey nor fancy nor beauty.

These makers of plays are of Broadway even before first they come to Broadway. What Broadway is and what Broadway stands for, they too are and they too stand for. The spirit of their early training has been not the quiet spirit of appropriate foods and appropriate guidance, appropriate books and schools and companions, but the spirit of street slang, of pert insolence, of opinionated bravado, of dollar divinity. And this latter training they have brought to Broadway, to the Broadway that glorifies it and venerates it, to the Broadway that is itself the crystallization of all the crude native superficialities in the arts — the Broadway that knows Schumann only as the inspiration of one of Planquette's duets in " The Chimes of Normandy," Titian as the colour of Billie Burke's hair, and Gourmont as a possible typographical error for the word signifying an omnivorous feeder.   But —

And here we engage the important point —

Broadway is honest.   It may be, in the way some of us estimate the things of this world, uncouth and shoddy and common, but it is without snobbishness, without spurious delicacy, without *simagrée* and false shame.   Its spirit is cheap, loud, but it doesn't pretend it otherwise.   And its people, though an absurd people, are withal a guileless one : the species that smokes cigars on the street, wears the watch-chain suspended from the lapel of the coat and regards Bernard Shaw and H. G. Wells as radicals — the species pistillate that would grandly demonstrate its familiarity with the French tongue by losing no opportunity to indulge itself in the droll luxury of pronouncing the name as Sarra Bairnhar, and that would emphasize its *bienséance* and unimpeachable status of lady by a *dégagé* pursing of its lips and elevating of its eyebrows as it sinks with a great display of nonchalance into a first-night orchestra chair. Yet these, intrinsically, are harmless histrionics, like those of so many little girls playing " society " in

[42]

their mothers' discarded ball gowns, and they fool nobody and but make the more emphatic the artlessness and *naïveté* that lie underneath the gaudy pink and purple satins and amazing *décolletés* and other such manifestations of the art of the Forty-fifth Street West Callot Sœurs and the other side-street Lanvins, Chéruits and Poirets. For, fundamentally, Broadway and its people, for all their untoward externals and protevangeliums, are children gullibly agape at a great Christmas-tree, dancing and shouting gleefully over the tinsel stars and salt-sprinkled cotton snow and cornucopias filled with lemon-drops. To them these things are as real: the tinsel stars destined to illumine the night of the world and the cornucopias crammed with sweet and candied apricots. . . . Broadway — a continuous performance of " Peter Pan " by an exceptionally bad provincial stock company.

Out of this childish quality, and doubtless because of it, there has come to the American stage what is the typical American drama, a drama which, though lacking all finish, all elegance, all worldly philosophy and penetration and distinction, is yet, and probably by virtue of these very defects, racy of the nation and emblematic of its attitude, its specious love of externals, its graceless hurry, gawky youth, somewhat immodest bluster and confidence. In this drama, the product of Broadway, there is neither the quality of reminiscence, for reminiscence is the privilege and estate of the mind's gentlemen, nor the quality of lives and loves greatly lived. Nor the quality of a heartache induced by something other than a declining stock market or the stage faithlessness of Florence Reed. Nor the quality of heart'sease imparted otherwise than through the spectacle of a seidlitz powder ingénue succumbing ultimately to the embrace of Mr. William Courtenay, or an alcoholic pickpocket yielding at length to the potent amending alchemy of peach jam and a canvas backdrop painted to represent a bucolic landscape.

But to such insight, but to such understanding and appreciation of and deep sympathy with the living things of this life, the Broadway playmaker, say what you will against him, makes no claim. He gives himself over, instead, to the things he does understand, and among these things the first is the way in which to amuse and entertain the countless Americans like himself who regard the theatre, and probably not without peculiar reason, as a refuge from art and literature, from beauty and truth. Who regard the theatre as an institution wherein the mirror that might be held to nature were vastly more entertainingly employed as an implement wherewith drolly to paddle the comique upon his antipodes, and wherein life is contemplated chiefly as an attempt to outwit the vindictive machinations of the New York police force. And the entertainments the Broadway playmaker thus provides his orchestra effigies and constituents are America's distinctive contributions to the dramatic records of the world, as distinctively American, if at once as distinctively unstimulating, inelegant and æsthetically haggard, as ice-cream soda, professional baseball, Billy Watson's Beef Trust and red-white-and-blue handkerchiefs. Making up in surface cleverness, novelty and breezy gait what they lack in the moods and manners of the finer dramaturgy, they excel, theatrically, by very reason of their deficiencies. For where it is a matter of loud farce or loud melodrama or trick comedy, the Broadway playmaker has proved in the last half dozen years that he knows more about his trade, and is a vastly more adroit craftsman, than his British or Continental competitor. He is more ingenious, more sagacious in the employment of his crude materials and still cruder philosophies, and the plays he builds are accordingly not only more ingenious plays than his rivals build abroad, but at the same time as indelibly and symbolically fragrant of the American attitude toward, and conception of, life and art and morals as the *Saturday Evening Post*.

The Broadway play, in short, is the representative American drama, and it is so regarded by the critics and publics of London and the capitals of continental Europe. The typical American play is not a play of the quality of " The Poor Little Rich Girl " nor " Old Lady 31 " nor " The Truth " nor " The New York Idea " (however much we might wish it were), but a play like " Kick In " or " Within the Law " or " It Pays to Advertise " or " Turn to the Right." They are not to be mistaken. For where " The Poor Little Rich Girl " might conceivably have been written by Barrie, where " Old Lady 31 " might have been written by Ludwig Fulda and " The Truth " by Alfred Capus and " The New York Idea " by de Caillavet and de Flers or G. K. Chesterton, it is pretty difficult to think of any one having written " Kick In " or " Within the Law " or " It Pays to Advertise " or " Turn to the Right " save an American. " The Faun," presented anonymously, might well have been attributed to a Continental like Molnar, but " Cheating Cheaters " would puzzle no one. Such plays are as undeniably and unmistakably American as " The Habit of a Lackey " is undeniably and unmistakably French or as " Maria Rosa " is Spanish or as " Riders to the Sea " is Irish or as " The Flag Lieutenant " is British or as " Anatol " is Viennese or " The Sea Gull " Russian.

Foreigners, the British frequently, the French occasionally and the Germans somewhat less occasionally, have attempted to imitate the Broadway-American play and to poor, if not indeed ridiculous, result. Such German imitations of the Broadway crook farce as Turzinsky and Stifter's " One Shouldn't Write Letters " have been as unhappy as such French imitations of Broadway melodrama as Bisson and Livet's " Nick Carter " or as such British imitations of the Broadway chaskleinismus as A. E. W. Mason's " For the Defence." Broadway is as exotically American as watermelon and the men's suits they make in Rochester, and its peculiar and individual dramaturgy cannot be duplicated by the foreigner any more than can the Bronx cocktail. The humour of Cartoonist Goldberg, the music of Irving Berlin, the drugstores of the Riker-Hegeman Company, the acting of Frank Craven, the House of Representatives, the Pittsburgh stogie, Beeman's Pepsin Chewing Gum, the mechanical barber-chair and the drama of George Cohan are each and all autoptically and incontrovertibly American, and the foreigner, if he would take them, must take them in their entirety, just as they stand, bone, fat and all, or leave them. They resist change, adaptation, tinkering. They are as saliently American, however greatly the foreigner may try to disguise them, as the drama of François de Curel and women's bangs slicked down with white of egg are French or as Wagner's operas and dill pickles are German.

Broadway, strident, half-cooked, credulous, unlearned and egregious, is the epitome of mob America and of mob America's view of art and letters. And its plays, not the plays of such as Avery Hopwood or Langdon Mitchell or Eleanor Gates or young Eugene O'Neill, are the plays that are most representatively American. That these plays are not always plays to the palate of the tenth American, that this one man out of every ten of his compatriots prefers probably the finer American efforts of such other writers for the national theatre as the Zoë Akins of " Papa " or the Edward Sheldon of at least " The Song of Songs " or the late C. M. S. MacLellan of " The Shirkers," does not alter the fact that they are, nevertheless and pertinently, the one genuine, blown-in-the-bottle contribution of the United States to the world's museum of show-shop literature and that they are in their way, and in their design and content, as valuable, significant and fruity to the international student of national characteristics as the flat-houses of Charlottenburg or a dinner with a French family in its home or a flirtation with a Chinese sing-song girl.

[47]

That these plays of Broadway are not more elegant specimens of dramatic literature may be, quite true, a matter for æsthetic regret, but this is not the point. At least not in this present chapter. The Ziegfeld " Follies " is the highest form of music show of its particular genre that the world knows today; it hits squarely the mark it aims at; and there's nothing to be gained lamenting the circumstance that, after all, it isn't an opera. The plays of George Cohan, by the same token, are the shrewdest specimens of their particular school that you will find anywhere along the coasts of the seven seas, and it is equally vain, and even sillier, to grumble that they have not been written by John Galsworthy. The trade of Broadway is the trade of turning out the Broadway-American play. And it knows its job superlatively well; and if that job is the jejune and humble one we know it to be, the knowledge must not obscure the fact that the Broadway playwriting type of American is still as considerable a virtuoso in his line as the Chicago beef-king type of American is in his or the Schenectady electro-mechanical type of American in his.

When the American of Broadway is a frank, natural and undissembling man, when he admits himself to be merely a good-natured dudeler and lays no pretence to the purple robes, when he confesses engagingly that he doesn't know a thing about the ologies and therapys and isms, nor about Mozart and Huysmans and Manet, nor about Sercial Madeira and butlers and finger bowls, when, in short, he strikes no spurious posture and seeks not to be a higher fellow than in actuality he is, he serves the American drama honourably and, for all his shortcomings, interestingly. For it is this playmaker who at intervals prosperously carries forward still another step the thoroughly American drama of such as Hoyt and Ade, who brings that drama a trifle closer to the national pulse, a trifle nearer to the national philosophy, a trifle more snugly, perhaps, within the bounds of a more finished technic. In this category we find such Broadway plays as Craven's "Too Many Cooks," as Smith's "Fortune Hunter," as Cohan's "Wallingford" and Megrue's "It Pays to Advertise." Of such is the real and more searching drama of the United States, of thrice the native authenticity of a dozen "Witching Hours," a dozen "Peter Grimms," a dozen "Cases of Becky" and "As a Man Thinks" and "Models" and "Bumpstead-Leighs" and other such pseudo-philosophical, pseudo-psychological, pseudo-metaphysical and pseudo-drawing-room pseudo-*opera*.

These latter *berceuses,* and numerous others like them, though all too commonly held up by the professors as high-water marks of the American dramaturgy, are in reality American plays only in so far as they have been written by Americans. But further than this they are no more genuinely American than Milwaukee. They are, for the most part, mere half-digested and shoddy apings and cuckooings of European plays, mere strivings of intellectual climbers to break into the select circle, mere antics of the bourgeoisie in Sunday clothes. When I say that it is the influence of Fifth Avenue, rather than the influence of Broadway, that has brought the real ill to the American drama, this is what I mean. I mean Fifth Avenue in the abstract, the Fifth Avenue complex in the physical and psychical composition of Sixth: the intellectual pusher, the toothpick user in the top hat, the Roget *littérateur,* the Phœnix Ingraham of the Broadway *beau monde,* the *halb-schopenhauer* of the Rialto's lettered élite, the Mezzofanti of Jack's. It is this influence and the playwriters it has bred that have brought to the native drama those qualities of fake and snobbery, of charlatanism and ankle-deep profundity, that have made the American drama a thing for mock and nose-fingering, a target for slapsticks and tin broadswords. It is this influence that causes the so-called dean of American dramatists to write, in the phrase of the late Charles Frohman, the way a negro talks, that causes the so-called wizard of American stage lore to tackle psychotherapeutical drama when his talent is really for the good, plain, old-fashioned melodramatical kind in which somebody beats Jack Dalton to the railroad trestle, that causes this and that writer for our theatre periodically to compose a society play in which the butler passes back and forth through the drawing-room on his way to answer the doorbell.

And it is this influence that, by so bringing these otherwise skilful writers for the stage to write of things foreign to them, at once takes them from that very field wherein they might do praiseworthy work and wherein they might labour to the greater good and greater estate of the native drama. For these misled writers are intrinsically clever fellows, some

of them vastly more so than some of their Broadway
confrères whose plays are numbered in the representative stage literature of our country; and that they
might further enrich and further develop this Broadway-American drama were they not so self-seduced
is only too plain, and only too regrettable. . . .
That the rooster a peacock would be, that chanticleer
would seek to control the source of all light, that the
modern Davids do put too much faith in the Goliath
fable!

To oppose the contention that these writers who
essay to break away from Broadway are to be com-
mended in that, coincidentally, they are making an
effort to inject a something finer, a something more
exalted and finished, into the Broadway-American
drama, is to argue (1) that the leopard can change
his spots and (2) that, having changed them, he may
be used conveniently as a checker-board. The one
thing above all others that the Broadway-American
drama does *not* need is finish. Its very crudity is the
thing that makes it what it is. It is this crudity, this
lack of polished writing and artistic exaltation, that
best serves it and permits it sharply to reflect its subject matter and its characters. The Broadway-
American drama and crudity are generically —
æsthetically, if you will — as inseparable as are
crudity and the American burlesque show, crudity
and Hindu music, crudity and the heavyweight prize-
fight or crudity and East Indian dancing. Take one
from the other and you have nothing left. To refine
the Broadway-American drama is to emasculate it,
to take the racy Americanism out of it and to fit it to

[51]

an inappropriate standard and formula. To refine the Broadway-American drama and to eliminate from it its crudity is to supplant the bladder in the burlesque show with a copy of the *Atlantic Monthly,* to add a bass viol and French horn to the Hindu orchestra, to make the prize-fighters perform like so many Bunthornes, and to persuade the East Indian ladies to don diapers.

But, even were the refinement of this drama a desideratum, the playwrights who have deserted the field for the more tony dramatic regions of polysyllables and metempsychosis and Pitts the butler, would in all probability be scarcely the souls for the job. What they would bring to the Broadway-American play would be not so much refinement in its genuine and tonic sense as refinement of the whimsical genre that they presently exhibit to us in their wares: that is, refinement translated in terms of a French maid, a mauve piano and some orange and magenta Elsie De Wolf sofa pillows. What they would bring to the Broadway-American play, further, would be the florid altiloquence which they mistake for fine writing and which presently contrives to make all their characters talk like a curtain-speech by an English actor.

On the other hand, were these Rialto exquisites to get back, so to speak, to the soil, were they to resist this impulse to strut and crow, were they to be again the men they truly are — not scholars nor men of letters nor bloods of the world of fashion, but dexterous fellows at stage writing withal — the Broadway-American play might benefit by their skill and experience, by the qualities they indubitably possess but which currently are buried deep under the layers of flourish and affectation. The Broadway-American drama is not always the *stupidaggine* and the despicable art form they and we are led by the macaronis of the forum to believe. It has its place, and a definite one, in American art and letters, just as have the excellent cartoons of Webster and McCutcheon and Briggs, the peculiarly indigenous and strikingly characteristic writings of E. W. Howe, and the humour of Ring Lardner and Helen Green. There is no more reason for the typical American writer of typical American plays to attempt to bring so-called politeness and literary atmosphere to Broadway than there is for the typical American writer of typical American songs to bring Verlaine and Swinburne to tin-pan alley. It is a double imitating to essay to make of the American drama a society drama, for American society is already a mere mimicking of English society. The typical American drama must be — and is — the drama of the typical American people. And the archtype of this people, already automatically and naturally exaggerated for the exaggeration vital to stage depictment, is the American people of Broadway.

# Chapter Four: Its Audiences

The late Paul Armstrong once submitted to H. L. Mencken and myself, as joint magazine editors, an article on American theatre audiences which, after hotly accusing the latter of everything from mere rats in the upper story to lycanthropy, sought for all time to establish their ignorance before the world and put them to complete abashed rout in a grand italicized *coda* that — after an inordinately long dash which seemed with sinister hush to beseech the reader to take aboard an extra lungful that he might be properly prepared for the final dumfounding fetch — gravely announced that where the average American audience did not know the difference between one Beethoven symphony and another, there was not a single peasant in all Germany who didn't know the whole nine by heart!  When we returned the manuscript to Armstrong with the affable comment that there probably was not a single peasant in all Germany who had ever heard of Beethoven, to say nothing of his symphonies, our friend became exceeding wroth and made high answer that he deemed our jest indeed ill-suited to his notabilia.  We tried subsequently to convince him of our perfect seriousness, but to no avail.  And he died still firmly convinced that we had been making unseemly mock of him.

I quote this memoir of the inner chamber because America is still full of Armstrongs who believe that the average American theatre audience is made up of blockheads where the average British or Continental audience is made up of professors of the true æsthetic. I have encountered such, personally and in their quill juices, among no end of American writers on the drama and no end of other persons connected both directly and indirectly with the world of the theatre. And each of them, it would appear, has imagined something to the effect that where the typical American who seeks the playhouse as a regular pastime cherishes Mr. Al Jolson and little else, the Frenchman of similar texture passionately dotes on Molière, the German Schiller, and the Englishman if not exactly Shakespeare, at least drama of the next best order. That the average American theatre audience is representative of the lowest breed of American, no one will deny; but the supposition that the analogous mob audiences of England and the Continent are comparatively of a vast superiority to the average native audience and that, unlike this audience, they are to a considerable degree representative of their countries' culture and fine feeling, is a something to jounce anyone who has slummed amongst them.

The mob audience, that is, the audience that supports the Broadways of the theatrical capitals and sub-capitals of the world, is much the same wherever one finds it. It is made up, for the most part, in England of the type of Englishman who reads *The Winning Post,* looks on Melville Gideon as a

greater composer than Purcell and Phil May as a
better satiric artist than Hogarth; in France of the
type of Frenchman who patronizes the Bouillons
Duval for their pies, reads Henri Bordeaux and
weeps copiously when the Mlle. Nelly Vignal comes
out in a purple light and with much eyelid flickering
sings " L'Eternelle Bohême "; in Germany of the
type of German who collects photographs of the
lady skaters in the Admirals'-Palast; and in Austria
of the type of Austrian who would walk several miles
to see the latest revue in the Raimund-theater, where
he wouldn't cross the street to get into the Carlthe-
ater on a pass.

The theory that the French mob audience flocks
ardently to the Comédie and the German mob audience to the chambers of Reinhardt is one of the
curious delusions fostered in America by those
ubiquitous native theatrical commentators who believe that because the foreign drama is a better and
finer drama than our own, the virtue of that drama
must be due to its appreciation and encouragement
by the general foreign theatre audiences. Nothing,
of course, could be further removed from the
truth. As many first-rate plays have been starved
to death in the popular theatres of Europe as
have been starved to death in the theatres of the
United States. Such substantial plays as Shaw's
" Cæsar and Cleopatra " and Pinero's " Thunderbolt " have failed as signally to woo the average
London auditorium dodo as such guano as " A Little Bit of Fluff " and " Mr. Wu " and the Vachell
stuff has succeeded. The American mob audience,

[56]

indeed, patronized "Cæsar and Cleopatra" in considerably larger numbers than the English. The average French audience permits De Curel or Jules Bois to run a scant two or three dozen nights and yells itself hoarse for a solid year over the bloodhounds in a Gallic version of "Sherlock Holmes," and over the long eyelashed M. Brulé as "Raffles," and over "Arsène Lupin." Antoine has lost almost as much on Shakespeare as the theatre that bears his name has made on cheap Cap Collier melodramas. The average German audience, promiscuously held up as a *kulturklatsch*, has caused four Hauptmann dramas in succession to be summarily removed from the stage for lack of patronage and has laughed such things as Hofmannsthal's "Christina's Homecoming" quickly into the discard, while it has pounded its palms in admiration over such colics as Walter Howard's transplanted tub-pounders and the same detective flapdoodle that has enthralled the Parisian. Reinhardt, to live at all, has had to rely on the frequent backing of social pushers. And Hauptmann was shouldered completely aside by the Berlin mob until a privately supported theatre gave him a hearing.

It is a well-known tradition of the American theatre that when the stage crew — that is, the scene shifters, electricians, et al.— pronounces a play good during the period of preliminary rehearsals, its judgment will invariably be subsequently concurred in and supported by the public. Thus, the voice of the stage crew is the voice of the American people. Three days before Mr. Augustus Thomas' "The

Copperhead " opened in the Shubert Theatre, where the Shuberts had given it a home after a number of other managers had denied it floor space in their respective emporia, the stage crew voted the play a magnificent opus. This was three days, as I have noted, before the première. The advance reports of the play promised not especially well. Such astute producers as Belasco and Tyler had rejected the manuscript when it was submitted by the author to them and such equally astute managers as Hopkins and Woods and Klaw and Erlanger had been reluctant to book it in their playhouses. And then when the play opened, the public, echoing the lofty *æsthetik* of the stage crew, paid in $14,000 the first week to see it and acclaim it a work of art! And the play turned out to be one of the big popular successes of a season.

If the American æsthetic demi-monde prefers Smith and Hazzard's " Turn to the Right " and Armstrong's " Jimmy Valentine," to Brieux's excellent " The Incubus," the average French audience prefers Rivoire and Bernard's " Mon Ami Teddy " and the adapted " Le Mystérieux Jimmy " to it no less. And if the average American audience prefers a so-called crook play like " Officer 666 " to the work of Langdon Mitchell, you may rest assured that the records show that the average German or Austrian levy similarly prefers a so-called crook play like " Der Herr Verteidiger " to the work of Max Halbe or Arthur Schnitzler. On the other side, if it be claimed for the German mob audience that it has been hospitable to the work of such meritorious fel-

[58]

lows as Thoma, for the French mob audience that it has applauded such as Feydeau, for the Austrian that it has liberally patronized such as Bahr and the British such as Birmingham, let it not be forgotten that the American mob audience has also visited success upon such of our own praiseworthy writers as Eleanor Gates, Avery Hopwood, Edward Knoblauch and Jesse Lynch Williams. But these instances of menagerie discrimination are as much the exception in Europe as they are in America. And the generalization from these exceptions is but another of the numerous nonsenses brewed by the local neo-Brunetières when they make bold to wade above their ankles in exotic waters.

The first-rate drama of England and the Continent has had as tough a road to travel as the American. And if it has flowered more beautifully in Europe than in America, that flowering has been due not to the attitude of the mob audience toward it, but, very simply, because it is possible for a European theatre manager to conduct his business upon a very much cheaper scale than the American manager and so give three or four plays a hearing — and take a gambler's chance on return — where the American manager can afford but a single risk. Thus, where a native producer like Mr. Hopkins is able, because of top-lofty actors' salaries, absurdly heavy theatre rental and the like, to take a flier on a single so-called unpopular and meritorious work like Berger's " Deluge," the Continental producer like Barnowski, with the same amount of money, is able to take a chance on four such pieces as Schnitzler's " Professor

Bernhardi," Hermann's "Little Yetta Gebert," Thoma's "Dear Relations" and Andreyev's "Students' Love." When, in this situation, it happens that the American public brings by its indifference summary failure to the Berger play and the Continental public by its indifference to Schnitzler, Thoma and Andreyev failure to these but, by its interest, success to Hermann, the leading heavies and genteel comedians of our local criticism, thinking only of the mob approbation of Hermann, proceed promptly to the conclusion that the American audience is a group of fribble goophers and the Continental a body of connoisseurs.

That the Berger play was no gold mine when produced in Europe and that the American mob audience which gave it the cold shoulder might, very probably, have patronized at least one of three other good plays had Mr. Hopkins, as Victor Barnowski, been able to afford that number, such professors fail to ponder. It cost Mr. Hopkins approximately five thousand dollars to produce "The Deluge" and these five thousand dollars were a complete loss. It cost Barnowski fifteen hundred dollars less than this amount to produce the four plays named, and his success with one of them gave him a profit of several thousands of dollars in the quadruple undertaking. If, therefore, Mr. Hopkins had been able for his five thousand dollars to produce, in addition to "The Deluge," three additional such commendable plays as those of Thoma, Hermann and Andreyev, it is assuredly a modest gambler's hazard that at least one of them, as in the instance of the Continental audience, might have met with a sufficiently remunerative response from the American audience. The whole thing is vastly less a consideration of public taste than of theatrical economics.

If the British mob audience has visited prosperity on " General John Regan " where the American mob audience visited failure, the American mob audience has visited prosperity on Galsworthy's " Justice " where the British mob audience visited failure. If the French mob audience has made a failure of Bernard Shaw where the American audience has made a comparative success, the American audience has made a failure of Alfred Capus where the French audience has made a comparative success. " Kismet " succeeds brilliantly in America and fails abjectly in France. " Know Thyself " succeeds brilliantly in France and fails dismally in America. Bahr's " Concert " succeeds as finely in America as in Germany, and Wedekind fails as quickly in Germany as in America. " Androcles and the Lion " goes no better in Austria than in America. And " The King " is as great a success in America as in France. . . . Two of one, gentlemen, and a half dozen of the other! . . . When the professors touch the caustic to the American yokelry for its lavish esteem of such mush as " Peg o' My Heart," do the solemn comedians not recall that the British yokelry has esteemed it no less? When the good souls decry the American mob's preference for such *méringue* as " The Rainbow," do they not remind themselves that the French admired equally Guinon and Bouchinet's play from which it was lifted. And when they deplore the American vulgarity which makes such an enormous success of " The Blue Mouse," do they forget that the same piece made a huge fortune out of a like vulgarity in Germany and Austria.

The average theatrical audience, the world over, is pretty much the same. Its response to such things as Hall Caine's " The Christian," " The Belle of New York," the Covent Garden " Cinderella " pantomime and the Cecil Raleigh-Henry Hamilton and Arthur Collins melopiece is, in general, as quick and as full in the shadows of St. Stephen's and Nelson's statue, and in the lights of the Rue de l'Opera and Unter den Linden, as in the shadows of the Times building and in the lights of Chicago's Loop. If, on the other hand, it in its American incarnation fails to grasp such a play as " Candida," the statistics show that in its French incarnation it laughed persistently at the wrong time when the play was produced in the Théâtre des Arts. And if it is locally immune to such a satire as " Where Ignorance Is Bliss," the records show that the satire has been not particularly contagious in its native Austria.

The popular playhouse is, in general and at bottom, not much less a *dépot* of wishwash in Europe than in America. For the intrinsic nature of the agglomerate European mob and the European mass ass is, after all, much of the kidney of the nature of our own mob and our own Hottentot. Both respond in the theatre as they respond out of that theatre. And both, in both situations, are sisters under their skins in the way of tastes and reactions, predilections and responsive gustos. On the streets the European mob whistles and hums the selfsame " Merry Widow " waltz, the selfsame " Puppchen," the selfsame " Un Peu d'Amour " and the selfsame " You're Here and I'm Here " that the American mob whistles and hums on its streets. And it buys the same three-for-five picture postcards showing the rear view of a fat soul with the legend " I'm glad to see you're back again," and the red and green portrait of the bald-headed family man bouncing an exotic chicken on his knee and observing that " Absence makes the heart grow fonder." And it, too, like our own people, coming home growling and grumpy from the working day, lights up with broad smiles in its crowded street-cars at the mere sight of a blinking, thumb-sucking, apple-faced baby.

The theory, therefore, that these European crowds are promptly metamorphosed into profound savants, cynics and art lovers the moment they enter a theatre, where the same American crowds remain so many gowks and doodles, offers a considerable enterprise for the critical digestion. The truth, of course, is that the average audience, whether in Europe or America, is generally alike as two derby hats. The average French audience, exactly as the average American audience, cares infinitely less for Paul Hervieu than for Harry Pilcer. And the average British audience admires George Robey, the highest salaried British comique, above Stephen Phillips exactly as the average American audience admires Fred Stone, the highest salaried American comique, above Percy Mackaye. And the average German audience prefers the Wintergarten to Reinhardt's

[63]

repertory theatre just as the average American audience prefers the Winter Garden to Grace George's repertory theatre.

Our average American theatre audiences are bad enough, the good Lord knows, but three weeks before the war swept the world I heard, in one of the principal theatres in one of the most cultured capitals of Europe, a typical European audience — the kind our professors are forever anointing with lavender flavours — shake the great chandelier with behemothine horse-laughs when a coquettish fat blonde in a low-cut red satin gown, hearing footsteps approach, guiltily exclaimed " My God! My husband! ", and when then there ambled on a tramp comedian juggling four brass spittoons. . . .

\* \* \*

Doubtless more insistently than any other native form of entertainment are the so-called William Hodge plays held up as deplorably emblematic of the average American audience's love for vulgarity and bad manners. This Hodge has made a great fortune, so say persons interested in such extrinsic matters, out of his annual laudation of God's Kansas and Ohio noblemen who drink out of the fingerbowl, pick their teeth with the oyster fork and clean their nails with the fruit knife; and he has thus provided unfailing copy for the mugient professors in the matter of *bienséance* and punctilio. That this Hodge and his plays go to make up, true enough, a stewardship of boarding-house ethics, is readily agreed. But that this cheap breeding and the remunerative approbation thereof is peculiar to our American mob audience is far from the fact. Europe has its Hodges no less than we. Germany has its Engels, France its Galipaux, Austria its Anzengruber Ghirrardis, and England its Weedon Grossmiths. These pantaloons, if not entirely in outward appearance, are yet Hodges in essence and comparative æsthetic, and their vulgarities are not greatly less to the palates of their respective national audiences than is the vulgarity of Hodge to the palate of our own.

The mob success of Hodge in America, however, seems to me to be founded less, as is generally believed and maintained, on the cocky ill-breeding and procacity of the characters with which he is invariably associated than on the almanac brand of philosophy which he through these characters invariably expounds. The almost mythical proportions of the success achieved in this country by such professional sunshine brokers as Dr. Frank Crane, Walt Mason, Orison Swett Marden, Gerald Stanley Lee and Herbert Kaufman and such members of the allied sorority as Frances Hodgson Burnett, Eleanor Porter, et al., prove beyond contention that the American public has an elastic stomach for this glad mush, and cannot get enough of it. And the Hodge, privy to the secret, simply strings along with the uplift pharmacopolists and gets rich, as they get rich, by dispensing in every other sentence of his play's dialogue some joy bolus or gloom antiseptic. A Hodge money-maker, therefore, is a thing all compact of such inspiriting philosophies as " Every cloud has a silver lining," " The darkest hour comes just before dawn," and "A smile in the heart will cure barber's-itch," and the American public goes to it like a cat to a saucer of warm milk.

# Chapter Five: Its Adaptations and Its Copeaus

Salient among the potentialities of Jacques Copeau's transplanted Théâtre du Vieux Colombier is the revealment in the United States of the modern French play in its uncensored flower, to the coincidental establishment and possible eventual domestic acceptance of the fact that the business of adaptation commonly visited upon that play is approximately as sensible as presenting Henry VIII in the light of an unconscionable hand-holder. The current promiscuous subtractions from the French play before that play is deemed fit for the American tooth are based upon two characteristic assumptions: first, in the instance of farce, that the Anglo-Saxon is incapable of viewing adultery save as tragedy, and second, in the instance of tragedy, that the Anglo-Saxon is incapable of viewing adultery save as grand opera. From these premises, both to a preponderant degree well-reasoned, are deduced the so-called adaptations which expound French farce to the American audience as a somewhat inscrutable procedure in which a man's mistress remains oddly enough a virgin, and the French problem play as a triumph of phylactery over physiology. As I have often pointed out, the dénouement is the kind of farce that proves that illegitimate babies are the result of promiscuous kissing, and the kind of problem plays that, in the original French, show us a man tiring of his wife and entering into a *liaison* with his wife's best friend and, in the adaptation, a man tiring of his wife's best friend and entering into a *liaison* with his wife.

It is a peculiarity of the Anglo-Saxon that he is able to conceive the seventh sin under no circumstances as a collaboration, but under all circumstances only as a plagiarism. Thus, it may figure for him as the basis of a melodramatic play in which a friendless young *émigrée* is decoyed upon docking by a plausible Neapolitan or in which the wife of a Union general is sardoued while in a fainting condition by an inebriated Confederate spy, but scarcely ever as a biological *scherzo*. It would seem, indeed, that its dramatic negotiation is comprehensible to him only in terms of aphasia, knock-out-drops or the Metropolitan orchestra. And it would seem, further, only to be æsthetically justifiable if expounded by a tenor and soprano neither of whom weighs less than two hundred and fifty pounds. He is able to swallow Tristan and Isolde, but he gags at de Caillavet's and de Flers' King Serge and Marthe Bourdier. He can work up an understanding smile for Musette and Marcel, but naught save a blush for Capus' Charlotte and her barrister. This attitude on his part makes for queer doings when the Continental play is prepared for Anglo-Saxon consumption, and not the least of these queer doings is a process of adaptation that, albeit unintentionally, converts such a play into what is unquestionably a much more scampish affair than it was before the surgeon set about his operation.[1]

The Frenchman regards a repeal of VII in either one of two sharply defined ways: (1) as a catastrophe, or (2) as a joke. And his plays treat of the subject from the one viewpoint or the other. The Anglo-Saxon, on the other hand, views the business primarily as a catastrophe — or professes so to view it — with the result that his plays must handle the topic either with a revolver or not at all. A frolic-

[1] *Contrary to the common opinion, the average American adaptation of a French play fails not because it deodorizes the original (and so perverts the original and makes it a thing ridiculous), but because it actually transforms the French play into a more immoral document than it was in its original form. True, this process is not intentional, but the result is the same. When, for example, the American adaptor adapts a liaison into a mere hot kiss, he forgets that his audience now sees the hot kiss in action where in the original manuscript, since it is impossible to depict a liaison in action upon the open stage, the French audience saw nothing. Again, when the American adaptor adapts a boudoir into a library he is compelled to make the characters go much further than in the original manuscript, since it is clearly out of the question for him in a library scene to resort to the original device of hiding from the audience the transgressions of the principal characters by a momentary dropping of the curtain. Still again, when the American adaptor turns a man's mistress into his aunt, he is guilty of an offensive Oedipus Rex complex in the minds of that considerable portion of his audience that has already read the plot of the original French play in the newspapers and magazines and somehow cannot entirely get it out of its mind. And still again, when the American adaptor adapts the illegitimate baby completely out of the play, the audience which would have forgiven the heroine's morals in the original manuscript on the ground that she was now a mother bursting with mother-love, in the adaptation views the heroine as a brazen, evil-minded and selfish hussy with no morals at all and absolutely no raison d'être.*

[69]

some regard of the situation has about it, to his mind, something decidedly indecent. This alone, of all the crimes and sins of the decalogue, is taboo; this alone must not be laughed at, even by way of simple theatre pastime. He sees nothing wrong in laughing himself half to death over wholesale murder (as in " Kismet ") or over wholesale thievery (as in " Officer 666 ") or over wholesale lying (as in " The Truth ") or over wholesale guile and deception (as in " Charley's Aunt ") or over wholesale lawlessness (as in " Turn to the Right "), but he draws a hard and fast line at Scarpia in cap and bells. And so he demands — or so at least the caterers to his theatrical taste imply he demands — that when sex intrudes upon his farce stage it be presented not as an act of physiology but as an act of Christian Science. From this insistence comes the locally adapted French farce like " Where There's a Will," in which, by the terms of a bequest, a lady must give birth to an heir in less than a year's time and to the consummation of that end persuades a strange young man to squeeze her hand, and the analogously edited French farce like " The Beautiful Adventure " in which a man hopelessly compromises a young woman by bidding her good-night at the threshold of her boudoir.

One merely increases nudity by draping it in transparent *négligé*. And, similarly, these adaptations increase, rather than decrease, the alleged indelicacies of the originals. They amount, intrinsically, to little more than an attempt to persuade Little Willie to believe in Santa Claus by dressing up his unmistak-

[70]

able pater in absorbent cotton and a maroon bath-robe. To imagine that the American theatregoer actually believes for one moment that a French husband is carrying on like a lunatic merely because his best friend has just chucked his wife under the chin, or that a French married woman is hysterically contemplating throwing herself out of the window because she has come in unexpectedly and, through the boudoir door, has caught sight of her husband and a gay actress from the Folies Bergère reading " La Suisse Famille Robinson," is surely going pretty far. The truth, of course, is that the American theatregoer is, in this situation, much like an eleven-year-old child whose parents still insist that the stork brings the baby: he isn't absolutely certain where the baby comes from, but he is absolutely certain that the stork has nothing whatever to do with the case; and so his mind plays upon a number of gipsy chords — and chiefly on the black keys. The result is curiosity, smirking, whispering behind the slate, stealing " Sapho " out of the book-case. And the further result is a *double entente* that, by the simple estimate of mathematics, is just twice as ententeful as a direct statement of fact. This is what Jacques Copeau should demonstrate, and eloquently, to the more discerning among American producers and to the more lettered members of the American public.

And also to the American censorship. Nothing, we are told, is inimical to the moral welfare if one can laugh at it. Why, then, a French farce must be adapted while a serious French play may be presented intact, is something of an enigma. From the

point of view of American morals, Bernstein's
" L'Elévation " is an exceptionally immoral play.  It
justifies adultery and makes a sympathetic hero and
heroine of the parties thereto.   And this justification
and canonization are accomplished with a ringing
and convincing rhetoric.   And yet it may be, and is,
presented in America without so much as a trace of
the blue pencil, where such a farce — a thing for
loud laughter alone — as de Caillavet's and de Flers'
" The King," which even in the original demonstrates
that adultery has its penalties, apparently may not be
presented save the adultery of the boudoir be modi-
fied to a mere clandestine playing footie under the
dining-room table.

The paradoxical morality of the entire business
becomes the more grotesque when one stops to consider that the American audience has become so tired
of the French triangle drama *á la* Bernstein in which
middle-aged married women go astray and convince
the American audience that there is ample moral
justification for such an excursion, that the American
audience will no longer bestow its custom upon that
drama, reserving its patronage instead for the French
triangle farce *á la* de Caillavet and de Flers in which
young unmarried women go astray and convince the
American audience that there is no moral justification
for the excursion.   The physiological dereliction of
Bernstein's Suzanne Cartier, defended, explained and
exonerated, it does not stomach, at least to the extent
of two dollars; the promiscuities of de Caillavet's
and de Flers' Therese Manix, undefended, unex-
plained and lightly laughed away, it rushes to observe

in such crowds that the play becomes one of the biggest successes of an entire season. The problem is as fertile in eccentricities as Richard Strauss' "A Hero's Career." The explanation, if there is an explanation, may possibly be discovered in the same native hypocrisy which, in another direction, permits the puritanical citizen unblushingly to enjoy a piping-hot Chicago, A. D., hula-hula dance if only the backdrop be painted up to represent Babylon, B. C., and in the matter closer to hand, permits him to revel in the forbidden joys of Paul de Kock provided only the adaptor tell him, with a wink, that the single ground for divorce in New York State is catching the whooping cough.

The projection of an honest light upon the current practises of adaptation is, as I see it, the leading white mark of the Copeau ambassadorship. To argue against this that since he plays in the French tongue he will be unable vividly to convince the American audience is to argue that since Mimi Aguglia played " Salome " in the Sicilian tongue she was unable to convince the American audience that the play was more sincere and effective in its authentic form than it would be were it adapted for the audiences of Miss Ruth Chatterton. The scene at the close of Act II of " The King," in its original form, is the same in all languages. Its meaning is quite as clear if the accompanying dialogue is in Sanskrit as if the words are written in English. The American who doesn't understand a single word of Russian has never yet failed, in an alien theatre, to comprehend perfectly the scene at the conclusion of the prologue to Tolstoi's "Resurrection." The American who doesn't know a single word of French has never yet, in Paris, failed to understand the central episodes of "The Habit of a Lackey" or "The Sacrifice" or "Have You Anything To Declare?"

Beyond this aspect of the Copeau enterprise, I can see little to intrigue the experienced critical attention. The local swallowing of the gentleman as an important Continental theatrical figure is, in its way, akin to the like gulping in the past of Gaby Deslys as a monarchical darling, Doctor Cook as a pole ferret and Granville Barker as a super-Stanislawsky, each as the result of a cunning press-agency. As a self-advertiser, Copeau's only rival in Paris in recent years has been Henry Bernstein. And still, with all his Yankee talents in this direction, the fact remains that he actually created a very meagre stir in France during the life of his local theatrical undertaking. There, as in New York, his original and most striking artistic accomplishments seemed to be confined very largely to performances in the pages of ornate pamphlets. As an obtainer of highly laudatory endorsements of himself, Copeau has indeed surpassed even Danderine. But though he is an unmistakably intelligent man and though, like Barker, he has a fine regard for the best dramatic literature of his country, he is at bottom, also like Barker, a mere artist of the theatre at second hand, a mere belated mimic of Reinhardt, Craig, Dumont, Stanislawsky and even the more remote Antoine (who produced Molière much as Copeau with a flourish now produces him), a man of the theatre who still loudly

[74]

revolts against those ideas of previous revolters which the latter revolters, after practical experiment, have already quietly and prosperously abandoned.

Copeau, during the one season of his theatre's career in Paris, became to Paris precisely what young Mr. Edward Goodman and his associates of the Washington Square Players became in their first season to New York. Copeau, in all truth, has done not one-half for the French theatre what the Washington Square Players have done for the American. The acting of his company is very, very much better — on this score there is of course no identification — but in the matter of ideas on scenic investiture and in the matter of drama and theory of dramatic interpretation he has shown himself by his accomplishments in no direction and in no degree superior to these, our own amateurs. Indeed, when one considers the vastly deeper treasury which he has had at his command, his accomplishments seem in comparison even less. What the somewhat excited gentleman of the *Times* contributes by way of choicest bouquet to Copeau, that " of two things he is very much the enemy: of a tradition that tends to mere routine, and of any disposition to exploit externalities — from tricks in scenery and costume to the personalities of favourite actors — at the expense of what is deeply true and beautiful," applies equally to the Washington Square Players, to the Provincetown Players and to the Neighbourhood Playhouse. Beautiful sentiments, praiseworthy promises. Indeed, the same beautiful sentiments, the same praiseworthy ideals, spoken by (and subsequently of) Augustin Daly in

[75]

his prospectus issued immediately after he had signed the lease for the Fifth Avenue Theatre back in 1869. (*Vide* " Life of Augustin Daly," by Joseph Francis Daly.)

Coming to Paris in the season of the life of the Théâtre du Vieux Colombier, I found at my hotel a note from the American playwright, Hopwood, for whose theatrical opinions I entertain a substantial respect, urging me to sojourn in the institution, as he already had done, and compare then impressions. I spent considerable time in the little theatre, saw several very intertesting plays and a great deal of nonsensical stage affectation, saw numerous very dull plays and a great deal more of empty stage posturing, and ended up by finding that Hopwood had found the same things and had come to the same conclusions — the conclusions similarly reached by the many Frenchmen of theatrical letters with whom the enterprise was discussed — the conclusions, to wit, (1) that Copeau was interesting to Paris chiefly because Paris was almost entirely ignorant of the new methods of the theatre long since familiar to the other nations, (2) that he was, in a way, the theatrical fad of the moment by virtue of his diplomacy in getting divers *jour d'abonnement* parties to give his theatre an off-boulevard air, and (3) that certain of the plays in his repertoire were intrinsically so very good that they were successful in triumphing over the affections which he was superimposing upon them.

The measure of sympathy that Copeau received from the Parisian was identical with the measure of sympathy the Washington Square Players have received from the New Yorker. And the Parisian in this regard was the same type of Parisian that the New Yorker in this regard is a New Yorker. Just as the anti-Broadway programs of the local amateurs gained for them the attention of a certain class of New Yorkers, so the anti-boulevard programs of Copeau gained for him the attention of that certain class of Parisians who, had they been New Yorkers, would have been the patrons of the Washington Square Players. But Copeau is no more a new Gordon Craig than Goodman of the local amateurs is a new Max Reinhardt. The simple truth about Copeau, indeed, is that he is a mere ghost of Craig in a windsor tie, Latin Quarter hat and baggy corduroy trousers. His voice is his master's voice. To ascertain this, all one need do is, first to read what he, in his various brochures, calls his " audacious " ideas on acting, scenery, the spirit of the author's work, et cetera, and then turn back to the files of Craig's " Mask " wherein, now somewhat covered with the dust of passing years, one may find the same ideas in very largely the same words. Or to Mr. Moderwell's book on " The Theatre of Today," more easily accessible, in which along toward page one hundred and twenty-eight one may balance Copeau's " Not nature, but release the spirit of the poet from the text of the play," with Craig's " Not nature, but look into the play of the poet." And Copeau's antagonism to realism and championship of style with Craig's " Not realism, but style." And Copeau's " Suppression of so-called stars " with Craig's " No personalities, but art." . . . What tempests of yesterday! But that, with all this, Copeau is a sagacious fellow remains impressed upon any one who has first laid a close eye to his ingenuous stage paraphernalia and then observed the canny way he rolls up his sleeves, puts in his hands and thoroughly convinces his clients that before their very eyes he is pulling out of the paraphernalia live artistic goldfish.

In his ideas of stage embellishment, Copeau strings along with the school which professes to believe that the best way to encourage the imagination is to do away with the scenery; in other words, that the most subtle way in which to make an audience imagine in turn such scenes as the forest in " As You Like It," the grounds adjoining Leonato's house in " Much Ado," the sea-coast in " Twelfth Night " and the big battle scene with Sheridan riding to the rescue in " Shenandoah," is not to set the stage with four different pictures representing respectively a forest, a garden, a sea-coast and a battlefield, but merely to fix up the stage with three tall white pillars, a couple of jars of nasturtium and some blue velvet portières. Now, this may be all very well, but I have as good an imagination as the next man and yet I submit that when the program tells me a scene is laid, as in " Les Fourberies de Scapin," in a public square in Naples and Copeau shows me a stage adorned only with a tapestry-hung balcony at the back, supported by a number of imitation marble columns and decorated with several pots of wisteria, what I imagine is less a public square in Naples than the lobby of the Hotel Astor.

The scenic affectations of such producers as Copeau are as empty, as futile and as absurd as, on the other hand, are the scenic affectations of such producers as Belasco. But, of the two schools, give me Belasco. Like many another, I feel rather in the manner of a kindergarten lad when Belasco asks me to imagine a gentleman's library by showing me a room filled to the ceilings with lavish sets of Genie Holzmeyer, Hall Caine and O. Henry and with passionate boudoir lamps and reproductions of " Aurora," " Paul and Virginia," Edwin Landseer's " Stag at Bay," Rosa Bonheur's " Horse Fair " and Millet's " Angelus " in gold flowered frames, but it is nevertheless much easier for me under such circumstances to get half-way to imagining a library than when Copeau lifts his curtain and discloses to my vision some pink curtains and green screens that, only five minutes before, he had requested me to imagine represented something like " Without the Castle, At Inverness."

The so-called New Scenery requires, for its complete practicability and effectiveness, the great and telling tact of a first-rate producer like Reinhardt. Without this tact, it becomes a mere affectation, a mere specious begging of the question, like giving a calico ball in wartime or patriotically knitting for the soldiers at a Wagner opera. As we get it most commonly in America, with but a few distinguished exceptions, the New Scenery is Art in the degree, and in the sense, that a new stack of foolscap is literature.

# Chapter Six: Its Music Shows

Of the baby talk that pervades the native journalistic theatrical criticism, not the least rich gurgle is that commonly achieved by the professors of blarney in the presence of a music show. Confronted with an exhibit of stripe slightly superior to that wherein the nephew palms off the burlesque queen as his wife on the rich uncle from Rio de Janeiro and the professors, a-gush with soft impeachments, are forthwith beheld sucking the cerebral forefinger and rolling the sheepy pupil. And bursting presently with the glows and agitations of the intoxicating amour, are further beheld seizing the hip and stepping forth in brave soprano to exclaim that here again, thank goodness, is a music show " that does not insult the intelligence."

There is in this ecstasy not, as one might believe, merely the customary desire to tickle the managers at whatever cost to critical honesty, but critical honesty itself, and of a very sincere and devout kidney. For these professors of the dailies still candidly esteem a catering to intelligence as a virtue in the music show, where almost everyone else, of course, appreciates that a music show that doesn't brazenly insult the intelligence is about as apposite and stimulating as an intellectual pretty girl, or going 'round on a carousel to the accompaniment of Bach's B minor mass, or getting a slant on with the kind of man who can tell off-hand exactly who Karl Gützlaff was, when and where he was born, and what were his chief works.

Although the American music show at its best has set a standard for the world, although in beauty, colour and movement it marks the one signal achievement of the American theatre, the truth is that its grave shortcoming is the presence, and even dominance, in it of the very intellectual quality so unctuously acclaimed by the journalists. This is the precise quality one goes to a music show to avoid, since the music show occupies to the theatre and drama the same relationship that the Café d'Harcourt occupies to the Luxembourg, that alcohol occupies to art: a convivial moment of forgetfulness, an opportunity to unbutton the waistcoat and get chummy with the garçons, a chance to cast off restraint and, in a measure, let fly at the chandelier. And the music show that best serves this end is certainly less the music show that vouchsafes a coherent plot, symmetrical lyrics and a musicianly score than the music show that vouchsafes in the stead of these some imbecile comic dialogue liberally interspersed with loud paddlings of the comedian's seat, some barroom *scherzi* and forty or fifty rosy-cheeked trollops.

More often, however, the native music show takes itself with deadly seriousness and the result is an American music show stage that actually is twice as intellectual as the American dramatic stage, and actually of three times the comparative philosophical depth. Take, in example, on the side of the native dramatic stage, the last four plays of Mr. Augustus Thomas, a playwright whose works may surely be accepted as more than merely a fair criterion of that stage's intellectual and philosophical attainments. These plays are (1) " As a Man Thinks," (2) " Indian Summer," (3) " Rio Grande " and (4) " The Copperhead." A scrutiny of the pneumatology of these *opera* produces the following creams. First, " As a Man Thinks " argues eloquently (a) that a woman who commits adultery is not as pure in morals as a woman who does not commit adultery, and (b) that if a married woman commits adultery, her husband, if he would thereafter live happily with her, had best keep his mind off the *faux pas*. Second, " Indian Summer " establishes the fact that a young woman is generally grateful to an elderly man whose self-sacrifices have helped her father out of serious trouble. Third, " Rio Grande " demonstrates (a) that a girl married to a man old enough to be her father sometimes seeks the love of a younger man, and (b) that her husband is angry when he finds out about it. And fourth, " The Copperhead " eulogizes as patriot and martyr a man who brings ruin to his household, sends his son to the grave despising him and causes his wife's death rather than betray a confidence, and who then eventually justifies himself in breaking the confidence on the ground that it threatens to keep his granddaughter from getting the job of teacher in the district school.

Take now, by way of example on the side of the musical stage, four typical shows presented during a like space of time, say such diversified exhibitions as " Madame Troubadour," " Adele," " Sari " and something by George Cohan.  A scrutiny here produces the following philosophies.  First, where " As a Man Thinks " argues for the double standard of sex, " Madame Troubadour " argues for the single standard (surely a less hackneyed argument and one, despite its age, more philosophically piquing), and, further, for the re-establishment of happy relations between the offending woman and her husband not through so spurious a sentimental tactic as that advanced by Mr. Thomas, but through the less sentimental and doubly sound motive advanced by Hervieu in " Connais Toi."  Second, where " Indian Summer " argues and endorses the sympathy of youth with age and age's sacrifices, " Adele," after the more searching philosophy of Nietzsche, argues at bottom that such sympathy on the part of youth stands in direct antithesis to the tonic passions which elevate the energy of human beings, that it thwarts the law of development and evolution, and that, contrary to the Thomas happy-ending *bouquet,* it is at once a multiplier of misery and a conservator of misery.  Third, where " Rio Grande " promulgates the news that a young girl married to an old man is often impelled to seek love elsewhere and that the inevitable result is unhappiness for the man, " Sari " admits the hoary platitude before the curtain goes up and proceeds to work out the philosophy in the more sophisticated terms of Boufflers and Voltaire.  And fourth, where " The Copperhead " interprets patriotism as being largely a logical reaction, a George

Cohan show, with infinitely more acumen, albeit possibly unintentional, interprets it as a reaction related less to logic than to pure feeling and emotion.

This comparison of the relative intellectuality of the serious drama and the music show may at first glance seem absurd; it may appear that virtues have been read into the latter by mere way of rounding out a desired paradox; but this is anything but true. Compare, without prejudice, the attitude toward national life, morals and ethical conduct of some such music show libretto as George Ade's " Sultan of Sulu " or Henry Blossom's " Yankee Consul " with the attitude of some such play as Thomas' " In Mizzoura " or Tarkington's and Street's " Country Cousin," and see which is the sharper, the more illuminating, and intrinsically the sounder. The theory that philosophy always wears whiskers and never smiles is a theory that dies hard, and therein we have the delusion that the lighter form of theatrical entertainment must of necessity be generically of a lesser thoughtfulness than the dramatic. Nevertheless, there is more thought, more acute observation of the contemporary times and manners, and more sagacious comment on life in a single music show book of the memorable Gilbert than in all the plays Sydney Grundy, R. C. Carton, Charles Klein, Louis N. Parker, Alfred Sutro and Charles Rann Kennedy ever wrote.

Such musical comedies as " Sari " are, true enough, the food of good diversion, but when I say that they yet fail to meet the exact and perfect requirements of the music show stage, I by no means overwhelm my-

[84]

self with an ambiguity. A musical comedy, at best, is the orphan of an opera. And the person who enjoys a musical comedy at its best is the person who would much rather hear an opera instead. The musical comedy is to this person what a snack in the Amiens station room is to the traveler on his way to Paris and dinner in the Café Viel : the unsatisfying best that is to be had at the moment. The better musical comedy, in a word, is not a thing in and of itself; it is a mere bridge, a mere bite of milk chocolate *in transitu,* a mere temporary pulling in the belt a couple of notches. Its place on the amusement stage — the stage of the popular theatre — is no more authentic than would be the place of intellectual drama on the operatic stage. The popular stage is rather the place for the sort of music show to which I have hitherto alluded, the show like " The Follies," or like the Winter Garden entertainments, or like Fred Stone's " Jack o' Lantern " and Hitchcock's " Hitchy-Koo " . . . The critic who goes to a music show to hear fine music and a rational theme is the critic who goes to the Metropolitan Opera House to look at Mary Garden's shape.

The trouble with our music show stage, to repeat, is that it is too greatly the toady to rhyme and reason, too greatly concerned with the extrinsic thing that passes Rialto-wise for intelligence. One does not visit a bordello to hear the duenna quote Karl Marx and the professor play Rimsky-Korsakoff. Nor does one go to a music show for a Björnson plot or the symphonic poems of a Liszt. One goes, very simply, to lay an eye to warmly lighted, brilliantly

coloured scenery and a chorus of good-looking
wenches led by some fancy imported houri, to some
such crazy drollery as Harry Watson's imitation of
famous men like Mr. Park, of Park and Tilford,
whom one always hears about but never sees, to
osculatory comedians climbing up the prima donna
on a step-ladder, to fat men and dancing girls and
makers of funny faces, and to Miss Justine Johnstone hopping over a brown canvas trench waving a
tin sword and putting to rout the Hun army.

Of all American music show producers, none is so
acutely privy to this secret as Mr. Ziegfeld. And
none, by the same mark, so successful. Where other
producers are forever making laborious efforts to get
sense into their shows, this Ziegfeld works might
and main to get sense *out* of his. To this end, he
often deliberately employs the very best dullest libret-
tists money can hire — men like Mr. George V.
Hobart, for example — to fashion his exhibits for
him. And the result is generally a show thoroughly
to the taste of the theatregoer who goes to a music
show for what it is and should be and who, just as
he has become studiously engrossed in Miss Pennington's masterly interpretation of the hoochie-coochie,
doesn't care to have his researches interrupted by the
intrusion of some plotty theorem. The libretto of a
Ziegfeld show does not, in the phrase of the journalists, insult the intelligence; it merely lets the intelligence sleep. And this is precisely what the libretto
of a good music show should do. Nor is this greatly
less true on the higher plane. The one striking flaw
in " The Chocolate Soldier " is the too provocative

book; it crowds altogether too harshly upon the beautiful score.

The success of a music show may be estimated in the degree that it caters discreetly to masculine wickedness. Since such wickedness has been aptly defined as the admiration of innocence, the show that most cunningly capitalizes innocence is the show that most prosperously serves its ends. It is in this very enterprise that Mr. Zeigfeld excels. Give him a woman whose Awakening to Spring occurred back in 1880 and who hasn't closed an eye since, and he can yet dress the archæologist up in such a manner and present her in such wise that she will have the aspect of Little Eva. The common error into which this impresario's critics fall lies in the belief that his exhibitions are successful because they palm off intrinsic innocence in the light of something slyly wicked. The truth of course is that his exhibitions are successful — doubtless the most uniformly successful in the world — for precisely the opposite reason. They palm off the intrinsically wicked as something slyly innocent. If, as Mr. Ziegfeld's critics imagine, his shows habitually succeed because of their complete lack of wickedness and correlative dominance of the quality of innocence, such a thoroughly innocent music show as " Iole," a show without so much as a trace of wickedness, would make twice the fortune of the " Follies."

But this Ziegfeld is not merely a virtuoso of virgins. Just as the enormous popularity and worldwide appeal of the " Merry Widow " waltz was clearly and astutely figured out by Dr. Stefan Deliya, of the Clinical Hospital of Vienna, in a pamphlet published in 1914 by A. W. Künast and Paul Knepler, so has Ziegfeld worked out and negotiated the Deliya findings in the matter of the musical accompaniments to his own shows. This secret of aphrodisiac rhythm is one of the underlying secrets of the success of both the " Follies " and the various " Frolics." Its presence makes a Ziegfeld show as inevitably as its absence unmakes a Morosco show or a Cort show. For the music show that is a music show is the show that loudly insults the intelligence and softly assaults the emotions.

# Chapter Seven: Its Criticism

The business of dramatic criticism, as expounded by the majority of our daily journals, is vigorously maintained to be less an affidavit of the adventures of a soul among masterpieces than the admirations of a soul among potboilers. One of the typical professors of this academy is the gentleman who signs himself " Alan Dale," and into the esoteric metaphysics of the craft this Mr. quasi-Dale has lately vouchsafed the curious a luculent peep.

For thirty years, this gentleman, with minor divergence, has fought fearlessly, courageously, and beyond power of threat or bribe, the battles of bad taste and mediocrity. With all the skill at his command he has addressed himself assiduously and with infrequent failure to the cultivation of the public's cheapest and most doggerel theatrical predilections. He has rarely side-stepped, rarely swerved, rarely faltered. No play might be so good that his slapstick was not zealously poised to explode a torpedo of low comedy against its trouser-seat; no play so bad that his syringe was not perched betimes to spray it with muscadine adjectives and cologned scare-marks. With the fine fervour of the believer in some holy cause, he has often stood far into the night before his mirror to compose his thumb at just the proper angle to his nose that his public in the morning might learn how sufficiently to deprecate such a writer as Hauptmann or Shaw or Galsworthy. And with a fervour not less ardent, he has synchronously sweated, with the sweat of a Mozart transcribing Allegri, over a dressing-room interview with some Casino houri that his public might appreciate exactly how much she loved her Spitz dog. Rare the young American writer of authentic promise who has not been airily waved away by Dale, and equally rare the young American player of authentic promise who has not been helped and encouraged, if a man, with the amiable reminder that his ears stuck out too much or, if a woman, with a polite wheeze on the similarity of her blonde hair to spaghetti. And even rarer still such young and sincerely striving organizations as the Washington Square or Provincetown Players that have not, at christening, been sprinkled with lordly and quipful pooh-poohs.

For thirty years this Mr. Dale has been tiptoeing up behind the drama and devilishly tipping its hat down over its eyes and pulling theatrical doorbells and tying tins to pedigreed tails and doubling up the bed-sheets and putting raisins on the fly-paper. And this cutting-up he has negotiated not in the sound spirit of a good healthy boy, but in the spirit of some kittenish Abigail, some sciatical papa larking with the youngsters on an eternal Allhallow-e'en. His comedy, on such occasions, has been not the light and lettered humour that coats the best of criticism nor yet the higher wit that sharpens it and forces it fully home, nor even yet the broad, robustious humour that at times best suits the appraisal of lowly things, but the sort of humour rather that proceeds from the comparison of something or other with a Limburger cheese or from some such observation as " ' Way Down Yeast ' ought to get a rise out of everybody." The sort of humour, in short, whose stock company has been made up largely of bad puns, the spelling of girl as " gell," the surrounding of every fourth word with quotation marks, such bits as " legs — er, oh I *beg* your pahdon — I *should* say ' limbs,' " a frequent allusion to prunes and to pinochle, and an employment of such terms as scrumptious and bong-tong.

In view of the manner in which Mr. Dale has over this long period conducted himself, in view of his shave-parlour jocosity and yokel affections of arbitership and apparent insensibility to the finer things of the American theatre, a considerable portion of even that humble West Forty-second Street audience at which his writings, and writings of a piece with his, are aimed, has been prone to regard him as one of the usual mirthless Andrews who, slightly to adapt Dr. Johnson, have taken up reviewing plays as a profession by which they may grow important and formidable at very small expense. Wherefore, picture the surprise of this Broadway element, the same element that has — and not improperly — at times barred Mr. Dale, the play reviewer, from its theatres, when this same Mr. Dale, turned playwright, discloses a play from his own hand, and a first play, that is seen in the main to be not only an intelligent, well-written and dignified piece of work, but, to boot, a play for the most part superior to the majority of Broadway-made *opera* which for three decades he has been reviewing. The conclusions, plainly enough, are two: either that Mr. Dale in his profession of play reviewer has for thirty years been selling his birthright for a mess of ashcan notoriety, or that the case of Mr. Dale establishes once more the fact that it is ever infinitely a more difficult thing to write good dramatic criticism than to write good drama. And of these conclusions, it is the second that at the moment intrigues me the more.

The unfortunate thing about this second conclusion is that, while it is perfectly sound, it has yet about it the pert aspect of silly paradox, an aspect which brings it skeptically to be smiled away and generally to be doubted as are doubted such equally sound, if superficially as dubious, conclusions that it is infinitely more tiring to watch a one-ring circus than a two-ring circus and that a cigar which tastes sweet in the shadow tastes bitter immediately one steps into the sunlight. And yet its integrity is not difficult of appraisal. In the history of the theatre and dramatic literature, how many the names of dramatic critics that, in comparison with the names of mere dramatists, have survived time? Think of more than a dozen or so, from Aristotle to Archer, if you can! For every hundred men who have succeeded in writing good drama you will be at pains to discover a single one who has succeeded in writing good dramatic criticism. And the ratio becomes all the more impressive when one considers that where one man tries to write drama a hundred men try to write criticism.

Criticism, for all the notable spicy epigrams to

the contrary, plainly calls upon a vastly higher series of attainments and accomplishments than playwriting. To write a single first-rate play, a man needs but to have observed and assimilated a single mood and phase of life and but the imaginative writing skill to present that single mood and phase of life in terms sufficiently of the theatre to make it sympathetically understandable to a variable number of first-rate persons grouped together in a single body. To write this fine play, the man need necessarily have no professional knowledge of what is precisely known as dramatic technique, and no experience and practice in its maneuvering, as witness, in example, the case in embryo of Dunsany or the case of Dr. Schnitzler or the case of John Galsworthy. Or, on a lower but nonetheless still authentic level, the case of the London typist who wrote the play called "Chains," the case of the Welsh lad who wrote "Change," and the data of several of the young Irish group. Further, to write this single memorable play, the man need not necessarily be widely traveled, widely read, deeply and broadly educated; he may indeed be as a sitter in a far and lonely tower and the play but the transcript of a single adventuring into the outer world. As witness the record of the remote and humble genius of a day, as Hastings alludes to him, who gave forth "Pathelin" and faded then from the earth. But to write a single piece of living, first-rate criticism of a first-rate play, a man must have within his grasp the sweep of all the literatures and all the traditions of all the stages of the world. This one piece of first-

rate criticism must automatically be builded upon
what remains of the man's findings from all the first-
rate criticism that has gone before, and it must, if it
would survive, be superior to such prevenient criticism. Any one may copy Brunetière and die the
next day unknown. To live on, one must improve
on him and advance him.

Dramatic criticism, unlike dramatic composition,
demands without exception a knowledge of all drama,
all human nature. It may not, like drama, concern
itself alone with an imaginative or photographic unit;
it must be all-embracing, all-comprehensive. The
writing of a " Romeo and Juliet " requires a very
great genius; but the writing of a criticism of a
" Romeo and Juliet " that shall endure as the play
endures, requires clearly a greater genius still. . . .
Dryden, by his own confession, found his critical
" Essay of Dramatic Poesy " a vastly more difficult
labour than his drama " All For Love." Pinero has
written some excellent plays, but his serious attempts
at dramatic criticism have been less than negligible.

Again, the dramatist, even in his appeal to souls of
the highest understanding, enjoys an obvious and distinct advantage over the critic in that he makes his
appeal to these persons in groups, that is to say, when
they are members of an organized crowd in a theatre,
subject to that sometimes confounding condition
which our friend Le Bon describes as the collective
mind and emotionalism, and so to a considerable
degree vacated — in this instance volitionally — of
individuality, mentality and clarity of percep-
tion. The critic, to the contrary, not only tackles

these souls of the highest understanding singly, one by one, but he tackles them, to boot, after their opinions on the drama in point have been more or less violently coloured in one direction or another through the group contagion above alluded to. Thus, where the dramatist deals directly with an audience automatically already halfway within his grip, and ready and eager to be impressed, the critic, on the other hand, deals indirectly with an audience automatically already halfway out of his grip, and indifferent and reluctant to be impressed. The dramatist tilts easily against human nature's softest spot, to wit, the emotions; the critic desperately against the toughest, to wit, the intellect.

Here, of course, I speak of the real criticism. But, dropping ten thousand stories to the Broadway species of " criticism," one still finds that, even on this lowly plane, what is true on the superior plane is here possibly also true. I say possibly, for I am at once sadly uninterested in and happily ignorant of both phases of this latter business, of both the Broadway criticism and the manufacture of the Broadway yokel-yanker, and so hesitate to present my opinions on either in too positive a manner. However, let us, for example in inquiry, take Mr. Dale's own case. Mr. Dale, in his play, " The Madonna of the Future," has written, as I have already noted, a piece very much above the Broadway general. It discloses a sense of style, a consistently polished manner, a feeling for word and phrase; its theme is viewed through the glasses of a man possessed of a certain pleasant measure of cultural background and expounded in well thought out and effective vein; its net impression is of a piece of writing designed by a presentable gentleman for a presentable audience. But turn now to the playwright's review of his own play, a criticism — it is surely fair to assume — he pondered carefully and executed with the best of cunning and skill at his beck. What does one find in this criticism? One finds, to put it mildly, not only nothing by way of genuine criticism, but absolutely nothing that would indicate its penman to have the remotest accurate notion about the merits and demerits of his own play or about the mould of drama with which it is in species identified or about the manner of dramatic writing which it negotiates or about even those perfectly patent elements in the popular drama out of whose womb certain of its own elements have been brought to life.

A single point in Mr. Dale's review of his play is amply illuminative of Mr. Dale's nescience as a play reviewer and will suffice to reveal the character of what precedes and follows. "I am going to credit myself," writes Mr. Dale in his review, "with a new idea — an idea up to the very moment — an idea that may seem shocking and startling — to those who like to be shocked and startled — but one that is being rushed along on the breeze of this portentous to-day. Has a woman, who has wealth, position, brilliant notions on the subject of bringing up a son to be a credit to his country — has this woman a right to become a mother without marriage, if she does not care for the idea of marriage and looks on it as superfluous?"

[96]

Aside from the somewhat peculiar literary complexion of the paragraph — and in passing observe, please, its solemn seriousness — what of it so far as it affords insight into Mr. Dale's equipment as a play reviewer, a reviewer of even the plays of Tin-Pot Alley? What of this amazing idea which Mr. Dale announces, with a warm self-congratulatory shake of the hand, to be "new," "up to the very momnet," "shocking" and "startling?" Ellen Key? Even Mr. Dale, further along in his personal *éloge*, reluctantly allows that the old girl toyed with it in her remote day. But old ideas, in all fairness, seem often new ideas when they are spread out upon the stage, and what of Mr. Dale's new, up-to-the-very-moment idea so far as is concerned the contemporary stage about which surely he ought, as a play reviewer, know? Has Mr. Dale forgotten the exposition of "Man and Superman" and the scene between Violet and Tanner and the latter's "They know you are right in their hearts, though they think themselves bound to blame you by their silly superstitions about morality and propriety and so forth. But I know, and the whole world really knows, though it dare not say so, that you were right to follow your instinct (i. e., to have a baby) ; that vitality and bravery are the greatest qualities a woman can have, and motherhood her solemn initiation into womanhood; and that the fact of your not being legally married matters not one scrap either to your own worth or to our real regard for you"? And much the same business in the same dramatist's subsequent "Getting Married"? And much the same business, in more solemn vein, in certain ironical passages of Schmidt-bonn's "Help! A Child Has Fallen From Heaven!" . . . And what of the al fresco fulminations of the Michaelis who stems from Key? And of Professor William Isaac Thomas? And of Mme. Anna Howard Shaw? Mr. Dale's new idea, he should in sooth know, is approximately as new as the idea of Stanley Houghton's "Hindle Wakes," which idea, unless I am much mistaken, Mr. Dale in his capacity of play reviewer held similarly to be "up-to-the-very-moment," "startling," et cetera, when the idea had already been done theatrically to death by David Graham Phillips in his play "The Worth of a Woman," and by Max Dreyer in "The Pastor's Daughter of Streladorf," and by Alfred Capus in "The Wounded Bird," and by Hjalmar Bergstrom in "Karen Borneman," and numerous others.

If meritorious plays like Mr. Dale's "Madonna of the Future" fail to prosper in the American popular theatre as feeble and empty plays like "The Lion and the Mouse" and "Common Clay" richly prosper, it is to no little degree, and by way of boomerang, the fault of such play reviewers to the American public as Mr. Dale. That these newspaper commentators have a wide influence on popular taste is as futile a denial as would be a disbelief in newspaper influence itself. And that they many of them debase this influence and that they many of them thereby grossly debase the popular taste by cadeting to that taste, but makes to defer on end the happier day when the popular theatre shall prefer the gentlemanly wit and humour of a play like Mr. Dale's to the cheap gutter badinage of certain other easily recalled plays which Mr. Dale and psuedo-critics like him have fulsomely recommended to the public.

# Chapter Eight: Its Imagination

The person who reads a play and takes himself then to see it acted in the theatre goes never to observe the superiority (or even parity) of the interpreters' imagination to his own, but rather always to observe in what remote degree the interpreters themselves, and the imagination of the interpreters, are successful in approaching the results of his own imagination. When, for example, a man reads the novel " A Prisoner of Zenda " and visualizes to himself its Flavia as a lovely compound of whipped cream and pansies, he enters a theatre assuredly not in the hope of seeing a heroine who surpasses — or even measures up to — his picture, but in the fond trust that the actress assigned to depict the heroine will not be quite so much the pie-face as usual. In a word, the theatre in such cases is a place to which one goes less in the hope of complete illusion than in the hope of being only half-way disillusioned.

To read a play, and to go then to the playhouse to see it acted, is much like marrying a woman before proposing to her. In reading a play, the imagination of the reader is limitless; in seeing the same play acted, his imagination is more often bounded in the front by a Mediterranean sky that nine times in ten is rich in grease-spots and fly-specks; on the right by the spectacle of a Sinn Feiner in shirt-sleeves making ready to shift the scenes; on the left by a marble villa through the centre canvas seam of which one detects the stage-manager chewing a slice of plug cut; and in the back by a catarrhal old party who persists in sticking the toe of his shoe simultaneously through the rear aperture in the seat and into the rear person of the spectator. Glancing up, in the library, from the printed book of the play, the dreaming vision may dally, without hindrance or interruption, in the sweet fields of fancy, and there sniff deliciously the scent of imaginative blooms. In the theatre, the dreaming vision is called upon to dally across a field of baldheads and there sniff deliciously the scent of Newbro's Herpicide. Imagination thrives upon solitude. In a crowd, it is dismayed, lost. One doesn't dream in Times Square.

Says Coleridge, " Stage presentations are to produce a sort of temporary half-faith, which the spectator encourages in himself and supports by a voluntary contribution on his own part, because he knows that it is at all times in his power to see the thing as it really is. Thus the true stage illusion as to a forest scene consists not in the mind's judging it to be a forest, but in its remission of the judgment that it is not a forest." The printed play, on the other hand, interposes no such obstacles to a complete faith. The forest scene which the reader pictures to himself is as real, and as vivid, as an actual forest; indeed, often much more vivid. And the lion prowling therein growls as ominously in his imagination as ever a live lion growled in actuality. In the theatre, the same person, viewing the forest scene, in effect says (subconsciously) to himself, " This, of course, isn't a forest, but they charged me two dollars and a twenty cent war tax to believe it is a forest, so, to get my money's worth, I shall for the next half hour believe it is a forest."    And as to the lion, " That would be a lion if it wasn't Phil Dwyer in a lion's skin, and that would be a lion's roar if it wasn't old Phil tooting a Klaxon auto-horn."

The library chair, however hard, has in it the illusion of a thousand Reinhardts, a thousand Bernhardts.    In its cozy harbour, the moon that sweeps over the desert in " Cæsar and Cleopatra " is a moon of far and wistful mysteries: not, as in the theatre, a partly visible bunchlight at R 2 with a purple gelatine slide in front of it.    In its warm recesses, the Kathi of " Old Heidelberg " is the Kathi of every man's youth, the Kathi with sunshine for hair and pink and white chamois for cheeks and forget-me-nots for eyes and lips that seem always to have just said If — the Kathi of long-ago, warm, starlit, university nights: not, as viewed upon the stage, an actress well beyond thirty-five in what is obviously a blonde wig and an equally obvious, and apparently painful, straight-front corset.    Sentiment, too, thrives on solitude.    The library lamp warms it into life as the sun warms to life the flowers.    It is slightly more than difficult to persuade sentiment to flit across one's fancy in the theatre when one considers under his conscience that the delicate stage address is synchronously to the two-hundred-and-ten pound mammal seated on one's right.

[102]

# ITS IMAGINATION

Sentiment is, very largely, the language of what might have been. Its feet of cobwebs rest most firmly on the empty air. The bachelor of forty, reading "When We Were Twenty-One" underneath the amber lamp, somehow sees himself as Dick Carewe, also bachelor of forty. He sees, somehow, Phyllis as the girl who once on a time meant so much to him, and hears somehow her "Again and always, I love you" as whispered not to Carewe but, down the years, to himself. And then he goes to the theatre. And there he holds Carewe in the bogus figure of Nat Goodwin, who somehow doesn't look at all as he does, and Phyllis — his Phyllis of unchanging nineteen — in the person of the cold, Hellenic Elliott, who may be beautiful in a way but who isn't his Phyllis of the amber lamp at all. The personal element, the element that was as an *apéritif* to his imagination in the reading of the play, is here in the theatre completely lacking. . . . And the draught from Exit No. 6 is hitting him in the back of the neck. . . . And a brat is bawling in the balcony. . . . And a sordid party in the next seat is telling his companion that business is awful rotten this year in Cincinnati. . . .

Love is beautiful in the degree that its depth makes it inarticulate. A love scene has melody for the reading ear since its song is sung only in the silences of the imagination. Heard in the theatre, and filtered through a modish Boston cockney on the female side and an equally tony Broadway patois on the male, it produces the effect of "Romeo and Juliet" played with a dull needle.

[103]

"Plays," wrote Anatole France, "show everything, and dispense with the imagination. . . . That is why they do not please dreamy and meditative minds. Such people love ideas only for the melodious echo which they awaken in themselves. . . . They prefer the active joy of reading rather than the passive pleasure of shows. . . . Every word of a book is a mysterious finger which touches a fibre of our brain like the string of a harp. . . . It is not so in the theatre. For the fine type used in printing, which leaves so much to be divined, is substituted men and women in whom there is nothing vague or mysterious. Everything there is exactly determined." Determined, and upset! There, the little Mimsey of "Peter Ibbetson" cruelly grows up to weigh one hundred and ninety odd pounds. There, Trilby is devastatingly revealed as a counterpart of Connie Ediss, and suffering from asthma. There, General Phil Sheridan, riding breathless over twenty miles to the Federal rescue, is presently disclosed to the flabbergasted patriotic gaze as being none other than the Confederate captain whose part ended in the previous act and who now seems to be masquerading in a Union suit. The roses that, in a reader's imagination, fill and perfume the garden of a Dorothy Vernon, on the stage are metamorphosed by the property man into two meticulously straight rows of stiff artificial geranium, somewhat soiled after the week's engagement in Pittsburgh. The lonely sail that in the glow of the library lamp glides smoothly across the horizon, on the stage is beheld hiccoughing its way against the backdrop. And the windblown hair of Hope Langham, standing at the rail of the coast steamer off the harbour of Bizerta, is held at the appropriate windblown length by a more or less visible black thread. And Prince Charming has to slide the little glass slipper into his pocket and slyly sneak out a more likely No. 7 B, as he kneels to adjust it to Cinderella's all too human foot. And one can detect the De Long hooks and eyes that fasten the fairy queen's tights. . . .

"The beautiful," said Baudelaire, "is something ardent and sad, something vague, lending a field to conjecture." The stage, in sooth, lends no such field. It sets as barriers before the vagrant imagination — as breakwaters against a gipsy fancy — a vast force of beauty snipers in the shape of such things as one-candle-power incandescent bulb fireflies, greenish maroon sunsets, actors in one-button dress waistcoats, and moons that flicker like a coquette's eyelid. It is of concrete things, mechanical things, painted things, all compact. So, indeed, that one may in a measure sympathize with Tolstoi's chill record of a trip to " Siegfried." " When I arrived," said Tolstoi, " an actor sat on the stage amid decorations intended to represent a cave and which, as is always the case, produced the less illusion the better they were constructed. He was dressed in woven tights, with a cloak of skins, wore a wig and an artificial beard, and with white, weak, genteel hands (his easy movements, and especially the shape of his stomach and his lack of muscle, revealed the actor) beat an impossible sword with an unnatural hammer in a way in which no one ever uses a hammer; and at the same time opening his mouth in a strange way, he sang something which was wholly incomprehensible."

For much of this annihilation of romance and illusion, of course, the theatre has but itself to blame. It becomes a doubled difficulty to believe that the fellow playing Hubert Sinclair, the fell knave, is the desperado the playwright would urge us imagine when in the very program of the play one glimpses a page advertisement displaying a halftone of Hubert in real life, seated peacefully in a chair with his three youngest children in his lap and with his wife bending affectionately over his bald head, and the meanwhile listening wistfully to a Victrola playing " Lead, Kindly Light."   And so, too, is it anything but easy to obey the dramatist and imagine the young woman playing the rôle of a convent girl as so innocent and unworldly that butter wouldn't melt in her mouth when the night before one has glimpsed the chicken in a somewhat elevated condition prancing around the dance floor of the Knickerbocker Grill with the actor playing the rôle of the bishop.   It is clearly but the restatement of platitude to suggest the damage that has been done the mimic world by these, its own tactics.   But illusion is a tender thing, as delicate as a violet leaf, and the slightest touch from earthy hands sends it packing; and once gone, it goes never to return.   It baffles recapture as a vanished dream baffles recapture, or as an indiscreet letter that has already been dropped into the box, or as a lovely maiden to whom once, in a wild, careless and unthinking moment, one has said " I love you," in German.

Illusion is to the theatre what half-lights are to the woman on the further side of thirty-two. The theatre is ever on the further side of thirty-two; it must needs envelop itself with the glamours of pretty fibberies and abstinence, with the pinks and ambers of wrinkle-hiding stratagems. Just as the characters to which the mind's eye gives birth in the still of the library are, after all, for all their vividness, but half sensed, half seen, so should the players of the stage sedulously maintain themselves apart from the public gaze and keep themselves ever remote, save when in the direct path of the footlights, from the curious and illusion-rending public eye. Juliet and Reisenweber's, D'Artagnan and a Buick, Little Red Riding Hood and Long Beach — these do not go well together. For the Juliet that floats on the smoke rings that curl to the library ceiling isn't somehow that kind of Juliet, and the D'Artagnan isn't that kind of D'Artagnan, and the Little Red Riding Hood isn't that kind of Little Red Riding Hood. The fair creatures of fancy do not wear Zippo Dress Shields; the heroes of the reading eye somehow or other do not seem to be the kind of men who find that Spearmint Chewing Gum is a wonderful aid to digestion.

\* \* \*

Nothing is more hypocritical than the averment that mere beauty should be held as of no substantial value in the theatre. We demand that dramatic prose be beautiful; that scenic investiture be beautiful; that stage lighting be beautiful; that the theatre auditorium be beautiful; why is it therefore not reasonable that we demand beauty as well in the players? No technical art, however ably developed or whatever the altitude of its stature, can provide the necessary and vital impulse to the Cleopatra of Bernard Shaw's fine play if the lady's face is wrinkled, if she is already at an age where she carries an umbrella on rainy days and eats an apple every night before retiring. An artist of the violin may have a face like a dollar watch and a figure like a boardwalk rolling-chair, but the difference between him and the actor is that he merely has to *play* the violin; he does not have to *look* like it.

The rotund Miss Rose Coghlan is a very able actress, an actress of exceeding technical felicity, yet all of Miss Coghlan's technical skill would be of no avail — as the lady herself would doubtless be the first to allow — in the absurdly simple rôle of Little Eva. It is impossible legitimately to get away from types in the theatre. And, analogously and coincidentally, it is impossible on many occasions to get away from the requirement for beauty. Beauty probably has meant more and has done more for the success of the theatre as an institution than has technical skill. The face of Mary Anderson drew tens of thousands to Shakespeare — and so assisted in the betterment of the theatre — where the technical art of Nance O'Neill in the same literature availed nothing. The beauty of Julia Marlowe gave birth to tens of thousands more of lovers of the theater than the greater technical skill of Lena Ashwell.

Nor am I here seeking to oppose the box-office

to art. The art of the theatre may only be encouraged and made to flourish by getting the mob into the theatre: it matters not how. If necessary, fool the mob, trick the mob — but get it somehow into the playhouse. Once there, one may do many things with it — and to the finer estate of the stage. Just as a child will not take castor oil, which will do it a great deal of good, unless its wise parents mix it with some exotic philtre and so pass it off on the unsuspecting youngster as a strawberry phosphate or a Sauterne cup or something of the sort — just so will the mob not take Shakespeare or anything else which will do it a great deal of good unless Shakespeare is mixed with something else and palmed off on the mob as a " show." But once Shakespeare, or any salutary literary tonic, is down, the mob cannot fail in time to perceive the beneficial results. Maybe not all the mob — that were altogether too much to hope for — but at least a portion of it. And so I repeat that a pretty face in Shakespeare will do more for the future upbuilding of an honourable theatre than perfect technique with a squint eye and a Grand Street nose.

I do not, of course, mean to argue that the most vivid memories of the theatre are memories of such lovely and technically deficient creatures of the yesterdays as that stream of sunlight that fell on amber cut-glass and to which the gods gave at birth the name of Sandol Milliken, or that silver saucer of *marrons* and cream designated all too prosaically as Gladys Wallis, or the crystallized pastels with eyes the blue of overalls that the theatre knew as Vashti

[109]

Earl — I do not, as I say, mean to argue that such as these linger in the mind longer than the less lovely and vastly more skilled Modjeskas and Janet Achurches and Clara Morrises. I do not mean to argue that this is the case for the simple reason that, melancholy though it be, the matter is too obvious to need arguing. . . . One somehow remembers the little blue flowers on the Saint Cloud road more vividly and with more pleasure than the great Tomb of Napoleon.

I should like to pretend that beauty does not prejudice me in its favor — I appreciate that such a confession weaken's one's professional standing — but I find I am less successful in the pretense than many of my colleagues. Than bald perfection nothing is more ugly. Mere perfect technique in acting leaves one as cold as mere perfect technique in writing. In acting, beauty lends that to technique which a fine viewpoint and a wayward fancy lend to writing: the cocktail, the reflective vista, the string instruments. For the mob, Bernhardt; for the *connoisseur,* Duse.

The manuscript of a fine play is literature. When that manuscript is taken into the democratic playhouse it is taken there, plainly enough, for purposes of sale to the greatest number. This theatre is a shop — a trade. Why not honestly, frankly, regard it as such? It is in this respect analogous to a popular magazine. A popular magazine buys a first-rate piece of literature from, let us say, Joseph Conrad. It realizes that it can not possibly sell the Conrad story to the mob in sufficiently large numbers on its merits as a first-rate piece of literature. So it indulges in the customary stratagem of surrounding the Conrad story with a lot of photographs of Palm Beach, ornate actresses, the interior of C. K. G. Billings' new house, Alfred Philippe Roll's paintings, Mrs. Philip Lydig and some nude sculpture — with, of course, a lithograph of a toothsome cutie by Harrison Fisher on the magazine cover. Lured thus by pretty pictures of pretty things, the unsuspecting reader is drawn into the Conrad trap and so, soon or late, in all probability made another captive by first-rate writing instead of by the literature of Robert W. Chambers or Elinor Glyn.

" A beautiful face," wrote Le Bruyère, " is of all spectacles the most beautiful." " The moral of art — beauty," observed the Goncourts. " A beautiful woman's head," said Baudelaire, " is one which makes one dream, in a confused manner, half pleasure and half sadness." And Aubert: " The impression produced on man by beauty is made of surprise, admiration, love, sympathy, desire and, generally, joy." Professor Brander Matthews probably remembers Yolande Wallace more vividly and with considerably greater pleasure than Robert Mantell's performance in " The Corsican Brothers." William Winter, down in his heart, probably retained a keener picture of Nina Farrington than of Eben Plympton in " Rose Michel." But neither of these estimable savants would admit it, any more than the Thaw jury would admit that it had been influenced less by the learned findings of Dr. Allan McLane Hamilton than by Evelyn Nesbit's little white lace baby-collar.

I write here what I write because I, though a considerably younger man than the venerables above mentioned, am (to quite a degree) just as much a hypocrite as they were and are. For the sake of my professional and critical standing, I frequently posture and prevaricate with an equally high gusto. Not infrequently I profess to believe that a very pretty girl is not so good an actress as she actually is, for the simple reason that I appreciate that were I to admit she was as good an actress as she actually is, nine out of every ten of my readers would protest that I had, in my estimate of her, been hornswoggled by her mere prettiness. But we — all of us — are gentlemen afraid. We scowl the scowl of pundits and babble hypocrisies and frauds. We thrust a hand into the bosoms of our Prince Alberts, strike an attitude like a statue in front of a small town post-office and mouth the fibs of flappers.

A great play is a great play before it is acted, all eloquent bosh to the contrary. Try to think of a single great stage play that is not at the same time a great library play. The notion that a fine reading drama is not necessarily a fine acting drama is nonsense. Try to think of an exception! This being true, why should we not, when such a play is lifted upon the stage, be privileged beauty in the playhouse where the call is for such beauty? " Les Hannetons " is a satiric comedy of the first water. It reads as well as it plays. Its heroine is supposed to be an exceptionally paradisaical party. Why profess to be as artistically satisfied with Mrs. Laurence Irving in the part as with, say, Peggy Rush? The finished technique of Mrs. Irving is, from the soundest critical viewpoint, not at all necessary to the interpretation of the rôle. The unfinished technique, the mere *ingénue* air and persuasive face, of the little Rush girl would bring to the rôle precisely what it requires. The belief that finished technique is to be admired in every acting rôle, regardless of the intrinsic nature of that rôle, is as incongruous as would be a belief that a great and versatile actress like Sarah Bernhardt could give a better performance of " Peg o' My Heart " than a more appetizing but immeasurably less talented actress like Laurette Taylor.

# Chapter Nine: Its Comedians

Gone with the day of musical comedy drinking songs the refrain whereof was sung to the accompaniment of bells secreted in the chorus' glasses, is gone the day of the musical comedy comedian whose comedic talent rested chiefly in a large putty nose periodically illuminated by a small red electric bulb. Twenty years and more have since flowed under the bridge of that nose, and these years have witnessed the birth of a new comique academy, an academy whose humour no longer consists entirely in sitting in a snug arm-chair which remains fastened to the comique's netherlands when he arises, nor in a voluminous pair of trousers hitched up under the chin with a large button on which is painted a white daisy.

Where, in that ancient day, any actor was regarded as a great comedian if only he had funny legs and ears over which he enjoyed muscular control, the pantaloon who in this more sophisticated era would woo the remunerative chuckle must be a fellow of somewhat more subtle stratagems and didoes. No longer, as in olden days, will an audience go into wild hysterics at the mere sight of a comedian walking out upon the stage wearing a wicker waste-paper basket for a hat, and with one shoe six sizes larger than the other. That glad epoch is now but a memory — the epoch of Thomas Q. Seabrooke and Arthur Dunn, of Francis Wilson and Frank Daniels, of De Wolf Hopper and Jimmie Powers, of Frank Moulan and Harry Bulger, of Jeff De Angelis, Sam Bernard, Jerome Sykes, Charlie Bigelow, D. L. Don, James Sullivan, Pete Dailey, Eddie Foy, Johnny Ray, Fred Frear, Harry Kelly, John T. Kelly — the epoch of " The Oolah," " Fleur-de-Lys," " A Dangerous Maid," " The Grand Vizier," " The Little Trooper," " The Begum," " The Little Host," " The Ameer," " The Idol's Eye," " Tobasco," " The Merry Monarch," " Wang," and " A Runaway Girl." Hopper falling down the collapsible stairway in " Panjandrum "; Daniels working his eyebrows in " The Wizard of the Nile "; Pete Dailey stroking his fur overcoat in " A Straight Tip " while a stagehand in the wings close by emitted cat mews; Francis Wilson getting mixed up with the suit of armour in " Erminie "; Jimmie Powers pretending he couldn't move his right leg from a certain spot and giving his knee extravagant wiggles in " The Messenger Boy " — they've all passed into the pigeon-holes, relics of a period when the musical comedy comedian was a comedian mostly in terms of a comic wig, a grotesque costume and a grand inaugural entrance effected by swinging a balloon across the backdrop with himself dangling therefrom, the seat of his trousers caught by the anchor.

The comedian of the present day may no longer content himself with so naïve a hocus-pocus. It no longer suffices that he merely engage as foil a mime half so tall as himself who shall, when the comedian seeks to locate him, sneak between the comedian's extended legs. Nor does it longer suffice that he merely don a wig the tuft of hair on the top of which responds sympathetically to a string concealed in his pocket. In the stead of such erstwhile guffaw breweries, the comedian of the present day, the comedian like Jolson or Hitchcock or George Bickel, must substitute a genuine sense of comic values and not a little acting ability. This newer school of harlequin must make the audience laugh without the aid of false cardboard ears, without the aid of a cow bell in the hands of the trap-drummer, without the help of such elaborate scenic stratagems as were vouchsafed the leading jackpuddings in the days of David Henderson and Rudolph Aronson.

It was probably not so difficult to be a comedian in those days. The loudest laugh Pete Dailey ever evoked might doubtless have been evoked by any layman in his audience, for this horse-laugh was begot not of Dailey's own effort but of the manœuvers of the unknown and unsung stage-hand whose job it nightly was — when the express train was expected imminently to thunder out over the trestle in " A Straight Tip," with Dailey meanwhile frantically trying to flag it — to shove out a sailboat. Thus, too, the loudest laugh that Francis Wilson evoked in all his long career came not from his own direct efforts, but from some stage-hand who, when Wilson (doomed, in " The Monks of Malabar," to die at the stroke of twelve) began counting the ominous strokes of the clock's bell and had counted

[116]

up to twelve — then made the thing strike thirteen.

Of course, there were comedians in those days, fellows like Dan Daly, who were ahead of their time, whose humour was spontaneous and whose methods were more after the current, and less artless, fashion. But in the bulk these posture-masters and pickle-herrings were a primitive lot, merry Andrews whose cardinal ideas of comedy were (1) an extravagant vibration of the knees and hands and noisy chattering of the teeth to indicate fear, (2) a device which caused a small green toy balloon to sprout from the comique's head when the latter was struck by the Prime Minister, (3) a piece of black cosmetic smeared on the lower front teeth, (4) a throne that would collapse when grandly sat upon, (5) a painting of an ancestor, hung in the Manor House, which would wink at the comique after he had imbibed a stoop of liquor and lead him, trembling, to place a whole pitcher of icewater upside down upon his head, thus causing a piece of ice to slide down his back, which piece of ice would resist his extravagant efforts to locate it, and (6) a tree painted on the scenery against which the comique might make to lean for support, a proceeding which would infallibly project the comique, and somewhat violently, upon his Little Jumbo.

That some of these masterpieces of ancient comedic histrionism were of jocund countenance, I do not presume to deny. The point is rather that their sponsors were comedians, not like the better comedians of today, in the intrinsic sense, but in the extrinsic. Where a present-day *bel esprit* like

[117]

Hitchcock, for example, is successful in making an audience laugh without the aid of make-up, the stage carpenter and a loaded cigar — in his more or less simple street clothes, so to speak — the comedian of yesterday was in the main unsuccessful unless he resorted to such spurious auxiliaries as the stuffing of big lumps of cotton into his tights to make his legs look like the legs of a gnarled and knobby rustic chair.

The comedian of today relies largely on the lines the librettist provides him, and employs, very often, a real histrionic skill and a practised voice inflexion to point them, to invest them with comic air, to draw out of them the last possible ounce of chuckle juice that they contain. The comedian of yesterday very often offered a performance that was one-tenth librettist to nine-tenths comedian, a performance which year in and year out was largely the same. This ancient scaramouch was wont to repeat one year a *soufflée* of all the tricks, grunts, mannerisms, postures and wheezes that had found favour with his audience the year before and the year before that and the decade or so before that. And the result was less a comedian appearing successively in different musical comedies than different musical comedies appearing successively in a comedian.

Thus, to take, for example, De Wolf Hopper, one was certain when one went to see "Wang" or "Panjandrum" or "Happyland" or "El Capitan" or "The Charlatan" or "Dr. Syntax" or any other musical comedy in which Mr. Hopper was starring that, whatever the nature of the libretto, Mr. Hopper would offer again his entire bag of tricks containing among other things (1) the picking of a carrot and some cherries off the hat of one of the women characters and the eating of them, (2) the elaborate preparation for a stupendous sneeze with the ultimate discharge of a diminutive sniffle, (3) the running of the scale with the voice, ending with a basso profundo rumble, (4) the burlesque classic dancing with the right hand held airily aloft and the left hand reaching swan-like to the rear, (5) the pit-a-pat little steps in imitation of the walk of a child, and the various equally familiar sister stratagems. Again, thus to take, for example, Jeff De Angelis, one might always expect to see, whatever the play in which the comedian was appearing, the familiar bundle of dodges beginning with the intricate tangling up of the legs during the flirtation with the leading lady and ending with the kissing of the entire chorus.

The buffoons of the yesterday were strangely stereotyped. Where, today, a comedian like Fred Stone labours ceaselessly to vary and to improve his performances — even beyond the variations vouchsafed him by his librettist — the comedian of the day of Benjamin Harrison and Grover Cleveland rested content year after year to repeat himself — and the himself he so repeated was more often than not a mere amalgam of the obvious antics of a circus clown. This saltimbanco had small feeling for wit, small talent or capacity for genuine burlesque. In the last four years, W. C. Fields, the comedian of the Ziegfeld "Follies," has devised more authentic, more novel and more amusing burlesque drolleries than such comedians as Arthur Dunn and Seabrooke and Charlie Bigelow and Jimmie Powers, all taken together, were able to negotiate in their entire footlight career.

When one recalls that the librettos provided the comedians of the yesterdays were four times in five of a humorous quality far surpassing the librettos provided the comedians of the modern day, the shortcomings of these bygone zanies become even the more vividly manifest. Unable often to get out of the comic libretto lines their full value, they were wont to resort to a concealment of this comedic and histrionic deficiency in costumery and wiggery the like of which was never seen on land or sea and in various elaborate mechanical expedients operated on their behalf by the stage-carpenter and his corps of assistants. In that era, for one Dan Daly who could make an audience laugh without making himself up to look like a retreat of the Russian army, there were a dozen who could not face an audience unless outfitted with a pair of green and yellow bloomers, a pink wig, an enormous scimitar and a mouth embellished on either side with sufficient rouge to make it look a foot wide. For one Harry Watson or George Bickel who today can make an audience laugh by a mere gesture, a mere roll of the eye, a mere twist of the features, there used to be two dozen who, to achieve a laugh of even one-half the proportion, were forced to resort to a costume that looked like the window of Schwartz's toy store the day before Christmas, and then, in that costume, turn a somersault and fall down a long flight of stairs.

[120]

# ITS COMEDIANS

The comedian of our American musical comedy has indeed improved with the passing of the years. Each season there is less and less in him of the clown of the sawdust ring, and more and more of the clever *farceur,* the droll wag, the inventive and even imaginative fellow. He is carrying forward the best traditions of the ambassadors to Folly, the traditions of such as Ward and Vokes, and Weber and Fields, and the little Rogers brother who is dead. He has forgotten — dismissed entirely — the obsolete, laborious and never-funny propaganda of the school of comique whose creed was a handkerchief containing a wet sponge and a large orange rosette sewed to the seat of the trousers.

# Chapter Ten: Its Motion Pictures

For all the dumfounding magnificences of its press-
agents' rhetoric, the motion picture, in this bloomy
day of its history, exhibits still nothing that visibly
lifts it above the artistic and æsthetic level of Chinese cooking or a German ballet. Though its
mechanism has indicated various degrees of im-
provement, though it has occasionally brought to
itself some of the work of men of first-rate endeavour
in the field of literature, though it has traveled to the
ends of the earth in successful search of lovely and
appropriate backgrounds, and though in the general
enterprise it has liberally expended millions of dollars, it remains yet precisely what it was in its in-
fancy: a mere ingenious mechanical toy for children.

It would seem to be the fashion to lay the blame
for this status quo, this monotonous left-right left-
right, of the cinema on the general illiteracy and
cheapness of its impresarios. But while these qualities are to be denied the latter not even by their most
friendly biographers, these same qualities have actually very little to do, whether the one way or the
other, with the motion picture's arrested development. Education, cultural experience and breeding
are intrinsically no more essential to the manufacture
of the motion picture, good or bad, than to the manu-

facture of pink chemises or vaudeville acts. These attributes are, in truth, a handicap. And the belief of certain persons that the motion picture might be made a finer and more beautiful thing, and something approaching to an art, did its governors have college degrees and social background is akin to the belief that Professor William Lyon Phelps and Mrs. Herman Oelrichs might make an art out of the view of an actor staring pop-eyed at the camera and thus registering alarm where the current Mosie Cohens and Isadore Rosenbergs succeed only in making a view of an actor staring pop-eyed at the camera and thus registering alarm.

The motion picture calls for culture and taste no more than the making of such mechanical playthings as walking bears and grunting dolls calls for these qualities, and for the same reason. The motion picture's appeal, by reason of the subjective nature of the motion picture as a form of diversion, is plainly enough not to the lover of music or of literature or of painting, or of any of the seven arts, but to the long-eared kind of person for whom P. T. Barnum devised the side-show: the person intrigued by an object in proportion as that object departs from the beauty of its type. That is, the kind of person who is curiously enchanted by the spectacle of abnormal twins, an immensely fat female, an excessively cadaverous male, a grotesquely tall Welshman, a woman with a beard, a dog-faced boy, a three-legged cow or some Bosco made up to look like the inside of a horse-hair sofa and nibbling at bananas polka-dotted to look like rattlesnakes. This, today, the typical

patron of the motion picture. This, the person who
thrills to sensationalized ugliness, to ingenuous
sleight-of-hand, to literature with the mumps, to
Rome in the days of its Los Angeles splendour and
Athens at the zenith of its Fort Lee glory. This,
the person to whom drama is impressive in the degree
that it divorces life, fancy in the degree that its
nymphs and fairies divorce diapers, and beauty in
the degree that it divorces almost everything save
the grounds of Mr. George Gould's Lakewood
home, a high waterfall, or a view of the Grand
Canyon with Douglas Fairbanks standing close to
the edge on one foot.

But these departures of the motion picture from
the pink of perfection are to be held critically against
the motion picture no more than similar departures
are to be held against a Montmartre Punch and Judy
show. For serious criticism of the motion picture
from the level of its press-agents' hysterias were assuredly as droll a tactic as bringing in James Huneker
to pass judgment on Anna Held taking a milk bath.
The only sound and fair critical attitude toward the
motion picture is the critical attitude assumed generally toward such analogous art forms as the coloured picture postcards of famous cathedrals with
the windows covered with small pieces of isinglass, as
the mailing cards containing such legends as " Don't
spit on the floor; remember the Johnstown Flood! ",
and as the Central Park species of Greek dancing
and the kind of drama in which the identity of the
principal character is eventually established through
the whereabouts of a mole. And it is for this rea-

son that what share of merit may properly be credited
to the motion picture may be credited alone to that
type of motion picture which candidly recognizes the
drollery of any other cinema principle or critical attitude, that is to say, the motion picture which sensibly
throws aside all pose and affectation and substitutes
an intentionally comic story for the promiscuous unintentionally comic one, and so relevantly exchanges
a slice of soft pie for Mr. Wallace Reid's celebrated
impersonation of the desperado of the plains with his
every eyelash carefully beaded and the Weber and
Heilbroner tag showing plainly at every blow of the
wind on the bottom of his new Georgette crêpe neck-
tie.

Not the swollen *opera* of such motion picture mes-
siahs as D. W. Griffith, but the simple slapstick pictures of such as Chaplin, represent the screen at its
most apposite and best. The performance in the
films of some such drama as Shakespeare's " Romeo
and Juliet " is doomed by virtue of the screen's inevitable pantomime to amount in effect to little more
than the playing of Gounod's " Roméo et Juliette "
on a silent piano. But this pantomime that here
deletes the presentation of its opulent poetry, and so
makes the whole proceeding as ridiculous as a dumb
man attempting to convey the beauties of Swinburne
by making faces, takes nothing from the motion picture slapstick comedy. The very shortcomings of
the cinema turn virtues in this latter. For where the
spoken word is absolutely essential to the intelligent
projection of any respectable drama not originally designed as a pantomime, it is as unnecessary to broad

low comedy as it is to the exposition of a fine painting or a beautiful piece of sculpture.   Falstaff in the
clothes-hamper and Toby at the pots are just as
comic, and just as Shakespearean, on the screen as
in the theatre or library.   But the Othellos and
Violas once they get onto the screen are no more the
Othellos and Violas of Shakespeare than a photograph of Corot's " Pastorale " is the " Pastorale "
of Corot.

Further, contrary to the general claim that the
motion picture offers a vastly greater vista to the
imagination than the stage, the truth is that it actually offers a vista immeasurably less great.   Where
the stage seeks merely to sprinkle water on the fertile
imagination and let it flower gracefully to its own ful-
ness, the screen drags out not only the sprinkling-can,
but the shovel, rake, clippers, flowers, flower pots
and fancy ribbons to boot.   It describes nothing,
suggests nothing, paints never a metaphor: it shows
everything, skin, flesh and liver.   If a country lad
halts his plough to dream wistfully of the world beyond the hills, is the director content that the lad's
dream be the nebulous dream that has crossed the
eyes of a hundred thousand lads before him?   Not
if the director can help it!   And so the lad's dream
becomes a rapid sequence of fade-ins and fade-outs
showing views of the Singer Building, the Forty-
second street Subway station at the rush hour, the
façade of Churchill's restaurant, and the lad in bank
president whiskers and a Prince Albert seated in a
mahogany office counting one hundred dollar bills.
Does a little orphan child wonder what Heaven is

[126]

like and, presto! — in the upper left hand corner of the screen appears some vacant New Jersey cow pasture full of extra girls in transparent white cheese-cloth dancing around an actor dressed up like James O'Neill, seated on a big red plush chair and representing God. Or does a character observe that his wrath is like unto the angry sea and — flash! — we are promptly given a view of the Atlantic Ocean.

Thus do the very scope of the motion picture and the irresistible temptations of that scope defeat the motion picture. Just as it is difficult to refrain from eating salted almonds once they are placed before one and once one has started, so is it difficult for the motion picture entrepreneurs to resist the flexibility of their medium. And it is because this flexibility works not, as the gradually increased flexibility of the dramatic stage has worked, for the better, but for the worse, that the motion picture is the obscene and melancholy gimcrack it is.

\* \* \*

That the motion picture might very easily be made better than it is, is of course perfectly obvious.[1]  But

[1] *The twenty leading axioms of the motion picture dramaturgy are as follows:*

1. *No country girl ever wears shoes or stockings.*
2. *All love-making at the seashore takes place on top of a rock close to the water's edge.*
3. *Through the windows of every business office in New York, one can see the Singer Building.*
4. *Wall Street men always receive news that they have lost their fortunes while their wives are giving balls.*
5. *All young girls have animal pets.*

that this betterment would fail to bring the motion picture even one-six hundredth of a peg up the ladder of even a pseudo-art is of course equally obvious. The motion picture is the result of a circumspect elimination of the principal attributes of four of the arts and a clever synthesis of the scum: it has re-

6. *All men who have mistresses present the latter with expensive pearl necklaces.*

7. *No man ever appears in his club save in evening clothes.*

8. *No blonde is ever wicked.*

9. *All foreign gentlemen wear Inverness coats.*

10. *All men, who, before their marriage, have led dissolute lives soon or late discover that their son's fiancée is their own illegitimate daughter.*

11. *In all card games, some one cheats.*

12. *An artist, going into the country to paint, always falls in love with a country maiden and, subsequently finding that his city fiancée has been false to him, marries the country maiden, the country maiden's brother in the third reel always suspecting the motives of the artist and being prevented from striking him by the country maiden.*

13. *All women powdering their faces before boudoir mirrors suddenly behold in the mirrors, to their wide-eyed horror, the villain entering the room.*

14. *In all fights in Western dance halls, the lamp is broken.*

15. *All evil plots in Russia are hatched by the Grand Duke Boris (assisted by an adventuress named Olga) and are ultimately set at naught by an artist named Serge.*

16. *All hallways contain grandfathers' clocks.*

17. *The German army, upon invading America, will make a bee-line for the home of some young blonde and concentrate its efforts in preventing the young blonde's fiancé from interfering while one of its sergeants imprints a kiss upon the mouth of the frantic and struggling maiden.*

18. *It is customary for all college students, whatever their alma mater, to have a Yale flag on the wall of their studies. This is especially true in the case of students at Harvard.*

19. *The only periodical ever to be found on the library tables in fashionable English country houses is the " Photoplay Magazine."*

20. *All river boats burn, and all yachts sink.*

[128]

moved style from literature, speech from drama, colour from painting, form and the third dimension from sculpture. Its relation to callæsthetics is the relation of chiropody to surgery. Its relation to the art of the theatre is akin to that of some suavely exploited lady of joy.

I except, as I have said, the frankly comical motion picture, for this type of picture, when it is well done — and it is sometimes extremely well done — is in its way a perfectly sound and estimable work, adroitly conceived, well written, well acted and ably projected. Appropriately " broad as ten thousand beeves at pasture," it depicts the low comedy of human nature from as much the viewpoint of Rabelais and Shakespeare, Swift and Balzac and Smollett and Fielding, as the law allows. The best writing that is being done for the motion pictures to-day — indeed the only writing worthy of the name — is the writing being done for these honestly and legitimately vulgar studies. Such so-called comics as " The Plumber," " The Submarine Pilot," " A Dog's Life " and the like are excellent things of their sort. They show imagination, a sharp eye to authentic comic values, a sharp sense of the fundamentals of certain phases of human nature; and, as broad vulgar low comedy, they are indeed not only tremendously superior at almost every point to much of the vulgar low comedy of such as Shakespeare, but to the bulk of the low comedy of the modern dramatic theatre.

But when we turn from this class of motion picture to the so-called feature pictures, we descend coincidentally from the honourably ridiculous to the sublimely imbecile. Nine times in ten the joint product of the efforts of some wretched scenario hack, some quondam tank-show stage director and some erstwhile pretty male counter-jumper or pantry sweetie, these pictures may no more be endured by a person civilized to the point of an occasional hair wash than the barroom slot melodeons that simultaneously render Balfe and one's weight.[1] Of unwitting ignorance, illiteracy, and stupidity all compact, they serve as overpowering propaganda for the further debasing of our native theatrical audiences' taste, and as a means of graduation to the dramatic stage of an increasingly ample corps of cheap melodrama and sweet slop writers, absurdly incompetent stage producers and bad actors. It is this school of

[1] *The widely held opinion that the motion pictures are the fatuous things they are primarily because their stories are composed by ill-paid, talentless hacks, is, however, absurd. Joseph Conrad's "Lord Jim" or "Heart of Darkness," made into a motion picture by Conrad himself, would prove on the screen as sorry stuff as the opera of any of the current hack scenario gentlemen. One can't play Hauptmann's "Hannele" in a tent nor Brahms' violin concerto on an oboe. One can't sense the spell of Salzburg through the windows of the Orient Express. The real trouble with the motion pictures lies not in their stories, but in the persons who produce those stories. These misguided persons imagine it to be the duty of their trade to elevate the motion pictures, to make of them a something better than they are and should be, when in point of fact they occupy in the amusement world the same position as dime novels, vaudeville shows, cabaret music, billiards and the free lunch. For such divertissements there is an ample, appropriate and remunerative public. Why, therefore, posture the motion pictures against the legitimate stage or the library? It is not essential to a bank's success that its teller be able to impart information on Xenophanes, Tschaikowsky and the spirochæte pallida.*

motion picture that buys a meritorious play like
" The Poor Little Rich Girl," pays many thousands
of dollars for it, spends many thousands of dollars
on scenery and fixings and many thousands more on
advertising, and then hires a fifty dollar a week ex-
dime novel writer to improve it by sticking in a prologue in which the little heroine, supposed in the
theme of the play to be burdened with a lonely and
tearful existence, is shown having a high and gay time
and laughing herself half to death with the compan-
ionable neighbours' children.   It is this kind of picture that shows Mr. Fairbanks, in the proud opus
hight " A Modern Musketeer," entering — so goes
the reading matter on the screen —" his gentlemen's
club "; that shows the American ambassador in the
European court scene of " The Goose Girl " senti-
mentally pulling a big American flag out of the pocket
of his evening coat at a state dinner and with it in his
hand addressing words of love to the grand duchess
seated at his left; that shows a motor-car with two
men on the box drawing up modishly in " Jack and
the Beanstalk " and then continues to show the two
men perched grandly, arms folded, in front while the
lady passenger gets out as best she can; that makes
Sapho an angel; and that shows, finally, in one of the
best known of New York picture theatres, a motion
picture in which, at the beginning, one sees a young
girl — " An orphan with no friend in the world,"
so goes the title — and in which, not five minutes
afterward, one beholds the same young girl, still an
orphan, " leaving for the country "— so the title explains —" with her father and mother."

[131]

The utter fatuity and drivelish content of these so-called feature films with their prodigally paid stars and directors exceed the imagination of one not privy to their gestures. On my table as I write, I have before me the literal accounts of some five hundred of these pictures culled from the several motion-picture trade-journals and expounding succinctly and brilliantly the literature of the art. For example, I quote first from these casual statistics the following chaste synopsis of a masterpiece released by the Goldwyn Company and entitled " Social Ambition ":

Vincent Manton is a successful business man possessed of a wife, whose sole passion is the attaining of social rank. In her lavish expenditure she reckons not her mate's financial limits and when the bank calls his loans, she turns from him with loathing and arranges an immediate divorce. His previous attempts to explain his finances had been met by her declaration of an ignorance of such. Yet, when Manton arranges to turn over the bulk of his shattered possessions she evinces an intimate knowledge of the schedules at the attorney's office.

Manton goes to Alaska, taking the shack of a former prospector as a place for abode. He frequents the dance hall of Big Dan Johnson, a resort more than well stocked with females. Rose, who is Dan's foster child and the apple of his eye, takes pity on Manton, in whose playing of " Home Sweet Home " on the piano she perceives the last despairing cry of a dying soul. She talks to Manton, who mistakes her for one of the gals, and for the presumed insult, Manton is badly beaten up. He is carried to his shack and later Rose comes to nurse him, bringing on an estrangement from Big Dan.

Gold is discovered on Manton's place, and with the way

to fortune in sight, he goes east with the misgivings of his new bride. His divorced wife makes a play for the man and he still possesses the old fascination for her until he discovers she is trying for his new fortune. So back to Alaska he goes to find his bride a mother and to tell her it's the West for them forever.

Second, the scenario (word for word) of an epic produced by the Graphic Film Company; title, " Moral Suicide ":

Richard Covington, an aged millionaire and stock broker and social leader of California, loyal to his motherless children, Waverly and Beatrice, becomes infatuated with Fay Hope, a woman with a past that is marred, and marries her in spite of the protests of his daughter. Contaminated by her mode of life and her associates, he loses his moral courage — commits moral suicide, as his daughter had predicted — and becomes estranged from his daughter Beatrice, who is ordered from her father's home by her stepmother, Fay Hope.

Lucky Travers, a New York gambler, follows Fay to California. He is her affinity, although she introduces him to Covington as her brother. As such he becomes the secretary of Covington. An old friend of the Covingtons recognizes Fay as a New York adventuress. This enrages Covington, who denounces the informant. It takes Covington some time to discover that he is a victim. His wife by her extravagance makes inroads on his fortune. Waverly, son of Covington, finding that Travers is infatuated with Fay, fires a shot at Travers. It hits Fay, killing her. Covington spends the remainder of his fortune in his effort to free Waverly from the charge of murder. Waverly is found to have been insane at the time of the killing and is sent to an asylum.

Bereft of family, friends and fortune, broken down in health and spirit, Covington drifts to New York, where he seeks employment. To prevent starvation he accepts the work of a sandwich man advertising a white light cabaret. Seeking refuge from the piercing winds of a winter's night, he visits the cabaret which he is advertising and finds Beatrice in the company of Travers and others drinking and acting in the manner of a wanton. Covington is horrified. He rushes to his daughter and begs her to leave the place with him. Beatrice, surprised at her father's appearance and his evident poverty, refuses to go. Covington tells her that fate has decreed that he was to advertise his own daughter's shame and that his punishment is too great to bear. Later Beatrice proves to her father that she is the same Beatrice as of yore and that her presence in the cabaret is a matter of duty to her country.

Third, a brief but illuminating record of the theme of a five-part drama called " Dolly Does Her Bit," by Miss Lucy Sarver, released by the Pathé Company and advertised as being " valuable propaganda for the Red Cross Drive." The record:

The story concerns the adventures of Dolly when she masquerades as a life-size doll, which was to have been raffled off in a Red Cross benefit, but which was broken. She cheers up the lonely life of a rich little cripple and is also the means of capturing a band of burglars. The helpless invalid thinks Dolly is the queen of the dolls come to life and the burglars kidnap her when she discovers them at work so she will not inform the authorities. But she escapes and causes their arrest.

He who isn't profoundly moved and doesn't help

the Red Cross after this eloquent plea has indeed a leather soul!

Fourth, a gem by Miss Bess Meredith, featuring a heavenly mime hight Monroe Salisbury and called " The Red, Red Heart ":

Rhoda Tuttle is taken west by her fiancé in an effort to cure her of extreme melancholy. While visiting at a friend's ranch she meets Kut-Le, an educated Indian who becomes devoted to her. Kut-Le knows the power of the desert to heal the ills of the mind and body, and kidnaps Rhoda. Under his care she gradually becomes robust, but desires to return to her friends. They, however, had searched tirelessly for her and finally find her and Kut-Le. De Witt, her fiancé, endeavors to shoot Kut-Le, believing him guilty of harming Rhoda. Here it is that the girl sees the noble spirit of the Indian, and forsaking her white friends and lover, returns to the arms of Kut-Le and the desert.

Next, an incalculably lovely opus called " Madame Jealousy: An Allegory," released by the Paramount Company. The opus:

Jealousy, looking through the mirror of Life, sees Charm and Valor happily married and decides to put Mischief at work to mar their contentment. She succeeds, and soon Sorrow, Treachery, and Rumor play their parts and cause trouble for the parents, Finance and Commerce. But soon Happiness is born to Charm and Jealousy and her companions are driven from the hearts of all.

" Flare-Up Sal," a drama by J. G. Hawks, produced by the Paramount Company, deals, so the statistics inform me, with

[135]

Sal, a waif of the plains, who earns the sobriquet of Flare-Up in the Loola-Bird dance hall, where she becomes a dancer and defender of her virtue, after deserting her foster-father who goes broke at the gaming table. Dandy Dave Hammond becomes enamored of Sal, but is restrained from any visible demonstration of his emotion. Meanwhile the stage coach is held up by the Red Rider, who apparently has no other purpose than to make prisoner a preacher journeying to the mining camp. The Red Rider carries the man of God off to his mountain cabin, and donning his clerical garb, goes in his stead to the camp. His arrival is the occasion of much hilarity from all, particularly Sal, whom the Rider has heard about and come to see. He holds services in the church, where it appears he is destined to become a fixture, until Dandy Dave takes a dislike to him, and attempts to give him the bum's rush. The Rider, however, is there with the rough stuff, it being his profession, and he proves to be one too many for the man of cards. The climax occurs within the dance hall when the Red Rider shoots out the lights and escapes with Sal, who meanwhile has come to regard him in a personal way.

In " Society for Sale," from the brain of Miss Ruby M. Ayres, and produced by the Triangle Company, I learn (again quoting verbatim) that

The action of the story starts within the first few feet of film, when the Honorable Billy goes broke and receives a financial offer to open the gates of society to a manikin in a modiste's shop. He later falls in love with the girl and proves himself very much of a man when put to the test, especially in the case of the supposed elopement of the girl with a notorious rounder who, incidentally, turns out to be her father. These two had not seen each other for many years and the girl's purpose in trying to get into society

[136]

was to investigate the stories she had heard about her parents before she revealed herself to him.

The story of " The Oldest Law," issued by the World Film, acquaints me, according to the documents, with

The daughter of a mountain hermit who comes to New York on the death of her father and secures a position as typist through the friendship of an elderly college professor. Just about the time she loses it, the professor dies and she is without funds. She spends her last three dollars for a dinner at the Claridge. Seated at another table is a young man who is arranging the details of his divorce from his wife. He follows her to the street and offers her the post as housekeeper of his fashionable apartment. As such she entertains his guests and is treated as his social equal.

The young man's wife opens a gambling house with the proceeds of her alimony and when a professional gambler fleeces her ex-husband she compels the crooked sport to return ex-hubby's I. O. U.'s, which she returns to him. Meantime, the mountain girl agrees to marry the crook if he will return ex-hubby's markers, being willing to sacrifice herself to save him from ruin. But as the ex-wife beats her to it in the saving process she is left free to marry the young man.

And, by way of a particularly fetching finale, I extract from the records the following nonesuch promulgated by the Fox Film Company with the eminent Theda Bara in the big rôle and called " The Soul of Buddha ":

The story opens in Java with English soldiers lolling about. Miss Bara is a flirty native girl, and her mother, fearing the worst, consecrates her to Buddha. She is taken to the high priest who has her swear to love no other than Buddha. In the sanctuary she chafes under the restraint and casts earthly eyes on the priest and almost seduces him. But he reminds her she is dedicated to the spirit and resents her blandishments.

There follows a sacred dance in honour of Buddha, at which is present an English major. Having fasted, she faints in his arms, and the priest cries that he has touched the flesh of a sacred maiden and must die. But the Englishman escapes with the girl on horseback, followed immediately by the priests, who happen to have saddled horses waiting for such a contingency. The Major takes her to English headquarters and quickly marries her. Then the pursuers enter.

The priest threatens she will pay the price and departs. To pacify the natives the Colonel demands the Major's resignation. The married couple go to Scotland and she tells her husband she cannot endure the bleak weather. He takes her back to her native village where a child is born to them. The priest kills the infant, leaving a " black hand " mark on its forehead. The husband then takes her to Paris, where she is melancholy. He must return to Scotland, and she elects to remain. She asks her maid to take her " where life and death are the same." Apache cellar and atmospheric dance. She is immediately inspired to do her native dance. Two apaches want to dance with her and she demands they fight for the privilege. Knives drawn, and she escapes with a theatrical manager who is there in search of types for his theatre. At her home the manager suggests she dance at his theatre and she consents.

The husband returns, shadowed by the High Priest, and protests against her dancing in public, but she scorns him, casting him off. At a reception given by a countess she cops her ladyship's husband for a lover. The countess comes to her home and pleads with her to give up her man and she laughs derisively. The priest emerges and tells the countess not to worry.

It is the night of her début as a public performer. Her husband has taken to drink and is a physical wreck. He pleads to be near her, even as her servant. She refuses and he promptly shoots himself. With her maid she thrusts the body in a couch chest as the manager and her count-lover rush in and inquire about the shot. She says she didn't hear any, and they do not detect the odor of freshly discharged gunpowder in the dressing room. There follows a sentimental scene with her count-lover. The priest marks her door with the sign of death. She is frightened, but brazens it out.

She then appears before the public with the stage set to represent a native shrine. After dancing she strides to the shrine, which materializes into the High Priest, who takes her in his arms, kisses her and stabs her to death.

\* \* \*

Turning to the motion picture serials, as they are known, I find an even greater artistic and literary quality. For example, Episode 10 of " Vengeance and the Woman " (Vitagraph), entitled " The Cavern of Terror," according to the synopsis shows us

Blake and his wife, Bess, captives in a cavern where they had sought to evade Black Jack and his gang. But as Bess was growing faint from want of food, Blake decides to run the gauntlet of the outlaws' fire and he and Bess come out into the open again. They are pursued by Black Jack, and finding the entrance to a tunnel, hide there. They are followed by the outlaws, but manage to make the other end first. There they are seen by some engineers who come to their rescue and a fight takes place between Black Jack's men and the workmen. One of the engineers is killed and in revenge the mountain side upon which the outlaws are standing is blasted and in a cloud of earth and rocks their forms are buried. But, unfortunately, Blake and Bess are caught in the upheaval, too, and their fate is left until the next episode.

In another episode of the same *chef d'oeuvre,* called " The Mountain of Devastation," we are informed that

We see Blake rescued from the wolves' gnawing at his body and carried to a nearby doctor. We see Bess escape from the outlaws by jumping to a tall tree and slipping down to her husband below. Next Black Jack and his gang dynamite a rock above Blake and Bess, but the pair miraculously escape and, finding a cable that will carry them to the other side of the mountain, they start swinging across the perilous gap in the mountain when Black Jack sees them and cuts the cable. The pair are then plunged into the rapids below.

Of Episode 2 in " The House of Hate " (Pathé), called " The Tiger's Eye," the announcement relates:

Just in the nick of time Gresham comes to Pearl's aid and saves her from being crushed to death in the yard of the munitions factory, where she was placed by the masked confederate of the hooded terror. They return to the house, and find the police investigating the murder of old man Waldon. While investigation is in progress, the masked kidnapper returns and as he is about to shoot Pearl from the window he is shot by Gresham. He lives long enough to tell that he was hired to kill the girl, but dies before he can divulge the name of his employer. Later that night, Pearl and Gresham arrange a trap, whereby they will be able to photograph the murderer of Waldon as he carries out his threat to rob the family safe. They place a camera in the head of a tiger rug and when the robber, who proves to be the hooded terror, is working on the combination of the safe, the flashlight explodes, allowing the hidden camera to perform its work. While Pearl is developing the film, the hooded terror, who has overpowered the detective on guard, enters the darkroom and the episode closes with the girl in imminent danger.

While Episode 10 in "The Hidden Hand" (Pathé), entitled "Cogs of Death," enravishes us with

The order procured from a magistrate by Abner Whitney for Doris and Verda to leave the house in which they live. The girls, accompanied by Jack Ramsay, throw themselves on the mercy of the housekeeper, who puts them up for the time being in her quarters. Abner Whitney has opened the safe and has taken the locket which is the only key to the secret packet, which is now in the possession of the Hidden Hand, who was almost killed by the fall of the chimney in the preceding episode, and has been revived by a resuscitating machine of his own invention after everything else had failed.

By a ruse, Dr. Scarley tricks Doris to come to his home, where he attempts to drug her, and in escaping from him the girl runs afoul of the Hidden Hand and his henchman, who pursue her until she, in desperation, jumps from a bridge into a coal car passing below. The impact of the fall stuns the girl and when the car comes to a stop the Hidden Hand has the car dumped into the coal pockets. The insensible girl is caught on the endless chain coal carrier and is about to be ground to pieces between the cog wheels when the episode fades out.

*   *   *

The way in which a moving picture play is written would seem to be something as follows: The president of the film company, desiring a new scenario at once, calls up his lawyer and asks the latter to find out for him whether or not there is a copyright on, let us say for example, " East Lynne." The lawyer finds out that there is no copyright on " East Lynne " and the president of the film company then realizes that his intuition was correct and that " East Lynne " will make an excellent moving picture. The president of the film company thereupon calls in a young man who once, in August, 1903, sold a story to a magazine and who is therefore now the head scenario writer of the organization, and bids the fellow forthwith turn " East Lynne " into a moving picture play. " We start work on it over at Fort Lee in a couple of hours, so you'd better get busy quick," the president of the film company remarks, and the scenario writer rushes out, buys a copy of the play, and, on page three, locates this convenient synopsis of the plot:

" Sir Francis Levison, a blasé man of fashion, commits a murder, for which an innocent man, Richard Hare, is suspected and arrested. Richard retains as counsel Archibald Carlyle, a rising young lawyer. Carlyle has just married Lady Isabel, the daughter of an Earl, who is in impoverished circumstances. After the marriage Lady Isabel's jealousy is wrought upon by the clandestine interviews between Barbara Hare, Richard's sister, and her husband, Archibald Carlyle. The interviews are merely concerning the defense of Richard in the murder trial; but Lady Isabel, in ignorance of this, misconstrues their purpose, and being goaded on by her lover, Levison, consents to an elopement with him.

" A few years pass, and Archibald Carlyle has secured a divorce from his wife and married Barbara Hare. In the meantime Lady Isabel, being badly treated by Levison, leaves him (he having neglected to keep his promise and make her his lawful wife). She learns of the serious illness of her little son, who is at the home of his father, Archibald Carlyle, and the latter's new wife, and determines to apply for the position of nurse for the little one, so that she can be by the bedside of her boy in his dying hours. Disguising herself as ' Madame Vine,' she secures the position, but overcome by the death-bed scene of her boy, she throws off her disguise and reveals herself to him as his mother. A reconciliation between Lady Isabel and Carlyle is brought about at the death-bed of Lady Isabel. The plot also shows how Sir Francis Levison meets his deserts by being brought to justice as the real murderer, thus securing the acquittal of Richard Hare."

This plot, the scenario-writer promptly makes over into a moving picture scenario as follows:

" Sir Francis Levison, a blasé man of fashion, derails the Northern Pacific Midnight Express at Savannah, Ga., for which crime an innocent man, Richard Hare, is suspected and arrested by a mysterious masked detective in the employ of the United

States Secret Service. Richard retains as counsel Archibald Carlyle, a rising young lawyer. Carlyle has just married Lady Isabel, the daughter of John D. Isabel, a great Wall Street financier who is now in impoverished circumstances. After the marriage (*Note: I think it would be a good idea to have the marriage take place in front of St. Patrick's Cathedral on a snowy day. This would make a classy set*), Lady Isabel's jealousy is wrought upon by the clandestine interviews in a lonely light-house between Barbara Hare, Richard's sister, and her husband, Archibald Carlyle. The interviews are merely concerning the defense of Richard in the derailment trial; but Lady Isabel, in ignorance of this, misconstrues their purpose, and being goaded on by her lover, Levison, consents to disguise herself that night as a gypsy and elope with him to Palm Beach in his high-power racing car. (*Note: I think this'll give a good chance for a pursuit scene.*)

" A few years pass and Archibald Carlyle has secured a divorce from his wife (*Note: This will make a swell court-room scene*) and has married Barbara Hare. In the meantime Lady Isabel, being badly treated by Levison, leaves him (he having neglected to keep his promise and make her his lawful wife). She learns of the serious illness of her little son, who is at George Gould's beautiful place in Lakewood (the home of the little son's father, Archibald Carlyle, and Archibald's new wife) and she determines to apply for the position of nurse so that she can be by the bedside of her boy in his dying hours. Disguising herself, therefore, as a Salvation

[144]

Army lassie, she secures the position but, overcome by the death-bed scene of her boy, she throws off her disguise and reveals herself to him as his mother. Barbara, overhearing all from behind a palm, dies of heart-disease; a reconciliation between Lady Isabel and Carlyle is brought about at the death-bed; Lady Isabel confronts Levison and reveals herself the mysterious masked agent of the United States Secret Service and, after a desperate hand-to-hand struggle (during which in a 'vision' Levison, who turns out to have been a white-slaver, sees again the wreck of the Midnight Express and repents), Lady Isabel shoots him dead."

This done, the scenario-writer hurries back with the script to the president, who renames the play " A Young Girl's Danger," shrewdly sends over to the Vitagraph offices to buy the railroad wreck scene used in a picture four years before, thus saving considerable money — and all is ready for the camera.

\* \* \*

Wherewith, I turn the case over to the jury.

# *Chapter Eleven: Its Actors*

Just as the average Broadway actress' notion of interpreting the rôle of an *ingénue* consists in putting her right hand back of her, cocking her head archly to one side and poking out her stomach, so the average Broadway actor's conception of a young man of fashion rests in draping the watch-chain at a bizarre angle, smearing the head with an extra quantity of hair salve, and buttoning only the lower button of the jacket. The mimetic art of Broadway is a direct descendant of the mimetic art practised by us youngsters around the age of ten in the loft of the family barn — an art in which the Devil was always portrayed by means of a red undershirt borrowed for the occasion from the gentleman employed to curry the horses; in which the organ-grinder was depicted by means of a bandanna and an ice-cream freezer; and for a glimpse of which the art lovers of the neighbourhood were taxed a variable number of pins.

The average histrionic performance on the average Broadway stage is related to acting in approximately the same degree that a certain familiar species of French pastry is related to Napoleon. When the average Broadway actor essays the interpretation of a character, his method of procedure would seem to be not to ponder that character's nature, appearance, demeanour, course of action and

[146]

attitude so much as the manner in which the actor who played a similar character in another play in the previous season interpreted the character. And what would appear to be true in the instance of this first actor would appear also to have been true in the instance of the actor whose earlier interpretation he copies. Thus, out of a sort of endless chain, are our interpretations and characterizations brought down to us — with the result that a socially well-placed bachelor is never under any circumstance presented to us save as a fellow given to an immoderate use of brandy and soda and a dinner coat which he periodically removes in view of the audience and for which he substitutes a velvet smoking jacket having a great deal of filigree work around the pockets, or an affluent old gentleman in no guise other than a creature given to lavish *boutonnieres,* the habit of mopping off his brow with his 'kerchief and the invariable practice of appearing upon the decks of ocean steamships in a light tan automobile duster.

As stereotyped and as recognizable as these are the pictures which the Broadway *grimaciers* present omnipresently to our vision in other directions. The coy young thing who interprets girlish cunning by pinning a false and very bouncy curl to the rear of her coiffure, by sitting on her right foot and by conducting herself generally like a Bromo Seltzer, is as familiar as the actor who pictures the heroic young lieutenant in the war plays, who comes out of battle for all the world as if a battle were a barber-shop, who plays the sentimental scenes mainly with his Adam's apple, and whose idea of depicting defiance is to stand with his feet wide apart. Equally familiar are the crook who indicates perturbation and nervousness by shifting his glance quickly from the occupants of Box A on the right to the occupants of Box B on the left, and who interprets his evil nature chiefly in terms of a collarless neck-band fastened conspicuously in front with a gold collar-button; the wronged wife who never enters the library or looks out of the window without clutching a portière, and who indicates her pent-up feeling of despondency by making two fists high in the air and coincidentally throwing back her shoulders; and the great novelist who, when wooing an idea, walks up and down the stage running his fingers through his hair, and who finally indicates that the inspiration has come to him by banging on the table.

That the actor is inevitably to blame for such humours is, doubtless, a contention somewhat — indeed, often far — removed from the facts. One recalls, for example, the incident of the stage producer who put on a piece in which that mirthful comique, Mr. Walter Jones, was playing the rôle of a tramp, and who, on the ground that he desired to inject a smart tone into the proceedings, ordered Jones to take his hands out of his pockets. That the stage producers are the really guilty parties on many occasions, one is not loath to believe. Themselves often alumni of the Broadway cabotinage, themselves often erstwhile interpreters of the rôle of Schuyler Van Rensselaer, the young society man who ubiquitously embellishes metropolitan drawing-rooms in a pair of white flannel trousers, these producers — now a rapidly fading order — are doubtless on more than one such occasion the Czolgozs, the Cocchis, the Lieutenant Beckers, the Leutgerts. It is they who murder further the corpse of what once might have been the art of acting; it is they who bring an actress to express indecision by placing her index finger alongside her right eye, who suggest that an actor register horror by staring out wide-eyed at Mr. James Metcalfe, and who order a juvenile to interpret the rôle of a college man in terms of a two-button fancy waistcoat, a resplendent hat band and a penchant for sitting on tables.

The acting one encounters in the duchy of the cinema, a species of posturing and anticking at which the superior snicker — and most often rightly — is not the only impoverished and absurd tactic upon the native democratic amusement platform. The stages of Broadway are generally as fragrant with the musks of incompetence and grotesquerie. Traditions have dug their claws so deeply into these stages — the worst traditions — that the screams of acting imagination and finesse may be heard nightly in the demesne. Huddled, an expatriate group, beyond the light of the Broadway stage door, stand the memories of Duse and Salvini, of the Ethel Barrymore that was and the Arnold Daly that is, while upon the warm and glowing boards within tread to dunderheaded poundings upon palms the unfinished, unlettered, unintelligible mountebanks of the moment, a dizzy procession of upstairs-tailors' dummies, pomaded witlings, broad "*a*"-d Mizzourians, vivified Punch and Judys. For one William Faversham who knows how to indicate an overpowering surprise, there are twenty rubber-stamp pantaloons whose idea of expressing the emotion is falling back into a chair with legs extended and arms flopping over the sides. And for one Lenore Ulrich who knows how to indicate tense suppressed emotion, there are a score of begauded blank cartridges who know no other way than to draw the mouth into a tight line, distend the nostrils and negotiate a hissing intake of breath. They obey not art, as Houssaye urged; they obey tradition. And not the best tradition, but the traditions of the cheap melodrama stages of the yesterdays.

One of the Goncourts wrote that " declamation may be noble, majestic and tragic with simplicity." How many actors realize the truth of this? How many, instead, seek to syringe a nobility, a majesty, a tragic beauty into their declamation by means of elaborate physical and vocal gymnastics, face-makings, chest-heavings, nose-blowings, gallery-gazings, bronchial *coups* and a blinding diamond ring? The average actor, as we lay eye to him in the popular theatre, is approximately as irrelevant, incompetent and immaterial as a love letter offered in evidence at a trial for automobile speeding. He has at his command not even the rudiments of his trade. Called upon to speak three simple words in French — words easily within the scope of even the humblest Swiss bus boy — he finds himself completely at sea. (In one of the productions currently on view in New York, an actor who has a record of something like thirty-five years of stage work behind him is sum-

moned to allude to the " Jardin de Plaisir." What
comes from his lips nightly is something that sounds
like Shardoon dee Place-ear.) Called upon to play
a few simple chords upon the piano, he is equally at
sea and must rely on someone stationed at a key-
board in the wings. Called upon to give a brief
turn with the foils, he has to resort to slapping his
foil against that of his equally inept opponent alter-
nately above his head and below his knees, for all the
world as if he were bouting with the broadsword.
Called upon to dance a few steps of the minuet in
a play of the yesterdays and the result is a cross
between a fox trot and a hanging onto a Subway
strap. Called upon to play a rôle requiring poise
and distinction, the issue is the spectacle of a man
who would seem to imagine that poise consists in affecting unconcern as to the disposition of the tails
of one's dress coat when one seats oneself, and that
an air of distinction may be conveyed by wearing an
immense gardenia and aloofly addressing the butler
over one's shoulder.

What, at bottom, the reason for all this, the
reason for this general incompetence of the actor?
It may be discovered, readily enough, in the impulse
of every aspirant to histrinoic honours to woo the
transitory laurel of the moment at the expense of the
more lasting and permanent award that comes out
of years of striving and study, out of years of careful
preparation and a gradually cumulative proficiency.
The actor thinks, in this, like a woman still single at
thirty: it is a case of getting a husband immediately
or never. He declines to content himself with an ar-

tistic investment in slow, but sure, Bethlehem Steel and rushes instead to the theory of the immediate millions of glory in some vague gold mine stock of the Curb Market. Said Max Beerbohm, himself brother to an actor and so privy to an actor's thoughts, "The actor's art is evanescent, and he must needs, therefore, be hectic in his desire for fame. Good books and good pictures are monuments which, once made, are always there and may take fresh garlands; but the actor's impersonation repeated, night after night, is a thing of no substance, exists not but from his lips, perishes with him. Other artists can afford to wait. But it is now or never with the actor." Of course, these are no new words; the Frenchmen spoke them many years before Beerbohm; but their probity remains through the ages. And thus it is that the actor, the good with the bad, views his career less as a career than as a careen, a taking at top speed of a perilous corner. His goal is not tomorrow, but tonight. The cheap applause of Broadway sings in his ears a lovelier music than the substantial commendation of the potential morrow. And so he rushes at his profession like a bargain-hunting woman, unprepared, wildly, groping blindly, indiscriminately. He is after not reputation so much as "a hit." His rainbow's end is in the next morning's newspaper reviews, appraisals as insecure as so many gilt chairs, as unlasting as white gloves. In all New York at this moment there are probably not more than five actors, at the most, out of all the many thousands, who can pronounce correctly the simple French word for "time," the simple German

word for " church," the simple Italian word for
" yesterday "— or who know how to pronounce
correctly the simple English word " poniard."
There are probably not more than four who have
ever read more than one play, at the most, by Gerhart Hauptmann, the dramatic genius of their time.
There are probably not more than three who can tell
you one single thing about the work of Giacosa, or
Pérez-Galdós, or Andreyev, or de Curel. There
are probably not more than two who have ever
studied the work of such excellent actors of their
period as Schroth or Guitry or August Lindberg, as
Madeline Roch or Julia Hakanson or even Marie
Löhr. And there is probably not more than one
who, on his sacred word of honour, can tell you
that he really understands what Ibsen's " The Wild
Duck " is about!

One wonders what the talented actors of the
American stage think of the countless mountebanks
who have invaded their profession and made of it
a thing for jest and ridicule. What does a man like
Drew think, or a man like Ditrichstein, or one like
Arnold Daly? This last, incidentally, is today
doubtless the foremost actor on the native stage. To
watch him is to be almost persuaded that there may
after all be something approaching to an art in the
business of performing a dramatic rôle, that acting
may after all call on somewhat higher qualifications
than a well-modulated speaking voice, a decent dress-
coat and amorous eyelashes. It is said by certain of
Daly's admirers that he is the actor he is because he
is an intelligent man; but this, of course, is merely the

stereotyped nonsense ever exuded when an actor reveals himself superior to the lack-lustre generality of
his fellows. Intelligence is no more essential to a
good actor than it is essential to a good sculptor or a
good Pullman porter. It is no more necessary that
Mr. Daly be able to distinguish between Pascal of
Clermont-Ferrand and Pascal of the Marigny or between Euclid's axiom of parallels and the Malthusian
doctrine than it is necessary for me to be able to distinguish between Cherryola rouge and Exovia paste
or to know how to take a headlong dive out of a
stage window after the manner of Don Cézar de
Bazan without breaking my neck.

Daly, I thoroughly believe, is the best actor
amongst us for the reason that if he is in sooth an
intelligent man he has the good sound actor-sense to
forget the fact the moment he passes into the stage
door. Thus, where certain of his competitors, pos-
sessing a modicum of intelligence, cannot resist the
vanity of parading that modicum upon the stage, to
the all too obvious embarrassment of the already perfectly thought out work of the author, Daly, with his
superior intelligence, sees the humour of his confrères' pea-fowlish carrying of cinders to New-
castle, appreciates that intelligence is the business of
the dramatist and humility before that intelligence
the business of the actor, and so makes of himself the
most genuinely intelligent and fully praiseworthy
actor in our entire theatre. When Daly walks upon
the stage, an audience may rest secure in the knowledge that what it is about to visualize is not an

[154]

actor's idea of an author's play, but an author's idea of an author's play.

There is much nonsense in the appraisal of histrionism. I myself, in the years of my novitiate, negotiated my full share. I recall now, and not without a mellow shaking of the head, what an engaging ass I must, in those days, have been: how seriously and Johnsonianly I was wont to analyze this and that acting performance and read into such performances things that must have both astonished and set to chuckling any actor foolish enough to read what I wrote. But at least I got over the practice of such juicy bosh. One does, in time. And it is therefore possible that the critical gentlemen of some of the current gazettes, in say ten years . . . twenty years . . . thirty . . .

Those of our American commentators who still view acting as an art (forgetting that such great actors as Coquelin and Salvini in their more lucid moments themselves hooted at the notion) are the same who in their critical writings on drama and literature allude to the so-called Continental viewpoint under the belief that the term signifies only something more or less directly related to indiscriminate venery. Upon the fine artists in musical composition, everyone agrees. Upon the fine artists in the interpretation of these compositions, everyone agrees. Upon the artists in paint and in marble and in drama and in literature, everyone agrees. If acting is an art, why cannot the supposed authorities similarly agree? Why the Duse — yes, Bernhardt

— no, Bernhardt — yes, Duse — no, pother? Why the mess over Mounet-Sully? Why the debates over Mansfield? Why the endless arguments over the Sicilian Aguglia? Why, in England, the yes and no over Beerbohm Tree? In Germany, over Alexander Moissi? In America, over Daly? If acting is an art, where the standards? And why is only Salvini greeted in the unanimous affirmative?

No one doubts that Beethoven and Brahms, that Kreisler and Hambourg, that Rembrandt and Rubens, that Michelangelo and Mercié, that Ibsen and Hauptmann, that Shakespeare and Conrad were and are artists. Why is there no unanimous agreement upon the high priests of histrionism? Plainly enough, for the same reason that there is no unanimous agreement upon race horses, prize fighters, ball players, one-step dancers or different brews of beer. Why otherwise, no greater concurrence in the appraisals of Mrs. Fiske, of Madame Simone (the French critics hold her a first-rate artist where the Anglo-Saxon critics merely snicker), of Emanuel Reicher (the German critics hold him a great actor; the American critics refuse to accept him), of even Sam Sothern (the British critics consider him an artist; the native critics consider him but a melancholious pantaloon)?

The truth is not difficult of plumbing. Art has the quality of universality; acting is more or less a thing sectional. Madame Morizumi is regarded as the greatest artist of the Japanese stage. She is venerated by the Japanese. In France or Germany or England or America her methods would, it is safe to

[156]

assume, be laughed at. On the other hand, a critic and scholar lately attached to the Japanese embassy in Washington once assured me that in his estimation Forbes-Robertson's Hamlet was, I quote his words, " as bad an example of acting as gives your American actors Mr. Robert Mantell and Mr. John E. Kellerd." The Hamlet of the celebrated Russian actor Glagolin would seem as poor a Hamlet to Western audiences as the Hamlet of E. H. Sothern would doubtless seem to Eastern. Dalmatoff's Quex won the highest and soundest critical praise of Petrograd. Yet it is recorded that a British critic who witnessed the actor's performance, and who further confessed that he had never seen Hare in the rôle and was so not prejudiced, and yet it is recorded that this critic observed that never had he seen a poorer performance of any rôle!

Acting is a thing almost as local as Rugby, baseball or any other sport. It is a pastime and, as such, open to local prejudices, tastes and predilections. The jury that sits in judgment upon it is like a cosmopolitan jury that sits upon woman's beauty; a jury that decides according to each of its twelve separate and divergent national standards. The world, without exception, recognizes the Fifth Symphony to be a great work of art. In all probability the greatest acting performance of more modern times was the performance of the central rôle in Sudermann's " Heimat " by Eleanora Duse. And yet several of the leading British critics asserted that Duse had not so much as touched the rôle — and yet the French critics to a man asserted that the perform-

ance could not be compared with that of Bernhardt
— and yet the Italian and Spanish critics asserted
that the performance of Bernhardt could not be compared with that of Duse — and yet a practised and
well educated and thoroughly trained Scandinavian
critic, stage director and actor, August Lindberg, if
I do not forget his name, asserted that *neither* Duse
nor Bernhardt had given a proper, an authentic, interpretation of the rôle!

While, of course, it is perfectly true that a work
of art is often, and may often, be debated, and eloquently, on both its sides, it is yet scarcely conceivable
that the master works of art, if they be debated at all,
be not debated eventually to a conclusion: a conclusion establishing them in their proper place and to
their proper stature and estate. That this conclusion is never reached in the matter of acting and acting performances is pertinent, significant. No more,
indeed, is the conclusion ever reached in the argument over the putting of Worcestershire sauce in
soup.

Réjane, an accomplished actress, confessed to a
pinch of strong smelling salts in her handkerchief
when asked by a friend how she achieved her dramatic flow of tears. The dramatist creates; it is im-
pertinence for the actor to attempt to usurp for himself the dramatist's right — this, the word of Coquelin. Zacconi, the illustrious Italian actor, once re-
marked that the best actor was that actor who remained constantly mindful of the prejudices of his
audiences and played to those prejudices. Enrique
Borras, the leading actor of the Comedia Theatre

of Madrid, has whispered that he cannot reproduce laughter on the stage unless he bethinks him at the relevant moment of the picture of a fat gentleman in a green suit falling down stairs.    D. W. Griffith, the motion picture director, in his early training of Mary Pickford used to employ some dozen or so flappers to rehearse in turn the scenes the Pickford was subsequently to play and from each of these flappers would appropriate for and visit upon the Pickford some effective girlish trick or cunning bit of business so that the Pickford, when finally she played the scene, became a composite of the prettiest little mannerisms of the experimental twelve.    And the Mae Marsh girl was made by the same process. . . . Well, well, it may be an art after all, may acting, but so then, too, by the same process of ratiocination, may be the laying of marquetry floors, the making of fine mince pies and the training of runners for the hundred-yard dash. . . .

# *Chapter Twelve: Its First Nights*

Nothing truer has ever been written than that the worth of a new play is decided for once and all by the attitude of the New York first-night audience. Contradiction fails; debate collapses; the fact remains. If the attitude of the New York first-night audience toward a new play is cold and sniffish, if it mocks and jeers at that play and makes sarcastic cracks in the lobby between the acts, if it refrains from bravos and applause, not all the critical eloquence of all the newspaper reviewers in New York City combined can succeed in proving to the skeptic that the play is a bad one.

The old pickle-herrings used to tell us that the best way to determine whether one's amber pipe-stem was genuine amber or merely imitation was to drop it into alcohol. If it melted into nothing, one might be certain that one hadn't been imposed upon and that the amber was the real thing. The same test may be applied to plays. If the play is a genuine play, it will not survive its first-night audience. The reason is simple enough. And here it is.

It is the boast of every regular New York first-nighter that he goes to the theatre, not in search of authentic drama, but, in his phrase, " just to be amused." A scrutiny of the statistics reveals clearly that he is not amused by good writing, nimble ideas, sharp characterization, searching philosophy and the component parts of good drama.   He is, to the contrary, amused primarily by such characterizations as rest in a forty-eight year old actress' depiction of a flapper by standing firmly on one foot and coyly, with head drooped, twisting the other in an outward direction, and by such philosophies as lie in a rebellious heroine's challenge to her cruel father that she didn't *ask* to be born.   To such stimuli the New York first-night audience seldom fails to echo.   Does the leading man tenderly observe that the heroine's hair is like a mass of burnished copper or that her teeth are like pearls, the effect is electric.   Does he, *per contra,* remark a trifle less conventionally that the fair heroine is like a bright flag flying in the breeze (as in Mr. Austin Strong's play " Bunny ") and the effect is palsy-stricken.   Does a pantaloon moistly ruminate that the heroine is like a broken flower tossed aside on the cruel highway of life there unnoticed and scorned to fade and wither and die, and the sniffles take on the volume of a New Hampshire hay-fever cantonment.   Does a mademoiselle look fixedly at the Brussels while some noble Bushman leans close to her right ear and murmurs therein that there are greater things after all than fame and fortune and a career — a tiny cottage all covered with roses and little children laughing and pulling at her apron-strings — and the ocular salt-drops flow like bock beer in West Street.

This innocence, this anæsthesia to somewhat less obvious stratagems and to fine drama and the things of fine drama, is not difficult to understand when one considers the personnel of the metropolitan first-night gathering. This latter is made up, for the most part, of the school that believes de Curel is what Della Fox used to wear on her forehead and that Brieux is, true enough, rather tasty, but on the whole not quite so palatable as Port du Salut. It is probably an eminently safe wager that, when the curtain lifts on the average Broadway *première,* there are not, at the very most, ten persons in the entire audience who know that Rüderer is not a brand of champagne, that Anatole France is not a French adaptation of Schnitzler and that Richard Strauss is not the junior partner of Abraham & Strauss' department store in Brooklyn. And, in the entire audience, there are in all probability not more than two or three, at the outside, who are able clearly to distinguish between Verdun and Verdi or J. S. Bach of Thuringia and J. S. Bache of the Wall Street firm of J. S. Bache & Co. The intellectual drive of the first-night gathering is pointed in directions other than these. For while that gathering may not be quite sure that the Waverly novels were not written by Scotti, it is thoroughly posted as to whether Geraldine Farrar loves her husband — and how much — and whether Bert Williams does or doesn't travel in the same car with the rest of the company. And while it may possibly confuse H. G. Wells with Trelawney, and Capus with a college lawn, it is quite certain in its ability to differentiate between Agnes and Egerton on the one hand and Vernon and Irene on the other.

[162]

This admirable sophistication and worldiness accounts for the attitude of the first-nighter toward the different grades of drama. For such a situation as marks, for example, the climax to Galsworthy's "The Mob," he cares nothing. To him, a situation is dramatic chiefly in the degree that the scene in which it is laid approaches (1) a boudoir, (2) the door leading to the boudoir, or (3) Police Headquarters. To him, a dialogue is dramatic in proportion to the number of times the one character issues to the other a summary invitation to go to hell. To him, fine writing is anything in which a well-tailored villain, on the point of raping the heroine, suddenly releases her from his embrace, drops his head and observes that one look into her eyes has convinced him that she is a good woman. The popular Broadway play, the play upon which the first-night audience bestows the tribute of its applause, is bounded on the north by the belief that authors always wear gold fountain-pens clamped conspicuously to their waistcoats, on the south by the theory that a detective, even on the hottest day in summer, never wears any kind of hat other than a derby, on the east by the idea that manliness consists solely in standing up as straight as a poker, and on the west by the notion that there is no form of habitation in the Riviera other than villas. The popular Broadway actor, the actor whom the first-night audience most loudly applauds, is that actor who wears braid three inches wide on his cutaway coat, who pronounces the word "valet" as if it were the noun designating the portion of landscape that lies between two hills, and who, every summer, has his photograph taken showing him sitting in his bathing suit on the beach at 'Sconset with his arm around Mr. Robert Hilliard.

The melodrama that wins the first-nighter's endorsement is based on the theory that the greatest crises in men's lives must inevitably occur after sundown. The farce, on the theory that all young women go to bed half-dressed. And the problem play, on the theory that when a wife runs away with another man, her husband views the event as a tragedy.

I doubt seriously that one may find anywhere in the civilized world a collection of one thousand persons so deficient in intelligence as the one thousand persons who go to constitute the average regular New York first-night audience. As I write these words, I am thinking of one man, a so-called typical regular first-nighter, who may fairly be taken as a criterion of his first-night brethren. This man (I have had a passing acquaintance with him for the fourteen years of my critical life) stands unmistakably for the metropolitan first-night audience. Know him, and you know the entire audience. Know his views and his tastes and his attitudes, and you know synchronously the views, tastes and attitudes of the nine hundred and ninety-nine persons who squat to his port and starboard. And what the nature of this man, this symbol and index? Let us see.

In the first place, this man has repeatedly expressed the opinion that the best play he has ever

[164]

seen was " Classmates." For the benefit of those who, in the turmoil of modern events, may have forgotten this epic, it may be mentioned that it was employed some years ago as a vehicle for Mr. Robert Edeson. The forgetful may further be prodded to memory by the reminder that it was in " Classmates " that Mr. Edeson got lost in a dense jungle swamp and, when eventually discovered and rescued, was seen to be wearing a pair of brand new and spotless patent leather boots.

In the second place, our first-night friend states, with an emphasis not to be mistaken, that the rottenest (the word is our friend's) show (the word is also our friend's) he ever saw was " The Thunderbolt " of Pinero. " Such stuff," he is in the habit of observing, " is too gloomy. It hasn't got enough action in it, enough wallop. It may be O. K. for reading such things, but when a man goes to the theatre he wants lively stuff with a punch."

Thirdly, our friend declares that, all things considered, his favourite playwright was the late Mr. Charles Klein. No one, he says, has in his estimation since been able to take the latter's place. " There was a fellow," says he, " who knew how to handle a deep idea without boring you. His ' Lion and the Mouse,' I'm willing to bet anything I got, will live."

I believe I have recorded enough about our friend brilliantly to illuminate the chambers of his soul. Say what you will about him, he is an honest man and no hypocrite. And his honestly expressed opinions are the deep-seated opinions of his first-night brothers who more often posture themselves in hypocritical and specious attitudes. These folk of the first-nights are as full of airs as a cantata, but get to the knuckle of them and you will find they regard any reference to Gatti Casazza an amazingly fine piece of wit and any man who wears a set of false whiskers and walks with his hand on his kidney a great character actor.

To the New York first-night audience, a piece of music is a good piece of music in the degree that there figure in its performance (1) the bass drum, (2) the snare drum, (3) the kettle drum, (4) the sand-paper and (5) the xylophone. Thus, something like " Bend Your Knees Like the Trees In the Breeze, Eloise " is a finer work of art than Brahms' scherzo in E flat minor. To the same gathering, a play is a piece of noble dramatic literature in proportion to the number of policemen in it. And to this audience, an actor is a capable actor in the degree that he is able to cover up his bald spot. It may be described, may this audience, as of the theatrical school that believes a burglar never enters a house save at night-time, that a butler always accompanies a visitor to the door of the drawing-room and stands there at attention until the visitor enters, that a poet always looks funny in evening clothes, and that no woman ever finally accepts a proposal of marriage without first making sure that she is standing in the exact centre of a room.

Among the plays in later years that the New York first-night audience has characterized as " rotten " have been Brieux's " The Affinity " (Les Hanne-

[166]

tons), Birmingham's " General John Regan," Molnar's " Where Ignorance Is Bliss," Ibsen's " John Gabriel Borkman," Hauptmann's " The Weavers," Pinero's " Wife Without a Smile," Chesterton's " Magic " and Berger's " The Deluge." Among the plays in later years that this same audience has characterized as " great " have been " Pollyanna," " Common Clay," " The Cinderella Man," " The Man Who Came Back," " The Warrens of Virginia," " Bought and Paid For," " The House of Glass " and " Here Comes the Bride." It has loudly applauded the score of " The Girl from Brazil " and has remained silent before the score of " Eva." It has cracked its palms over Beerbohm Tree in " Colonel Newcome " and has kept its thumbs in the arm-holes of its white satin waistcoats at the performance of Faversham in " Othello." It has discouraged a man like the Broadhurst of " Over the 'Phone " and encouraged a man like the Broadhurst of " Today." It has elevated the play in which the crook gets a smell of a homemade plum pudding and promptly reforms over the drama of Galsworthy and Harold Brighouse, the play in which the potwalloper from the red underwear belt puts the Four Hundred to social rout over the drama of Dunsany and Bahr.

Now, say what you will, this is no mean accomplishment. To believe that this condition of affairs might be brought about by *any* group of one thousand persons is to believe what is not true. The thing requires a very superior illiteracy, a cunning ignorance, a very virtuosity in tastelessness. No mere group of novices could conceivably succeed in so brilliant and complete an inartistic *tour de force*. The capacity for admiring a play like " Lilac Time " more than a play like " The Three Daughters of Monsieur Dupont " certainly does not come to one naturally, spontaneously. Such a thing seems impossible. It can come only after a sedulous, one might even say relentless and unswerving, avoidance of education and after an assiduous insensibility to cultural standards. The talent for believing Michael Morton a greater dramatist than Gerhart Hauptmann calls for no mere comparative lack of training: it demands a thorough and encompassing lack of training, a meticulous inappreciation of good literature, a long and faithful apprenticeship to the ninth-rate arts. And so it is that the first-night audience of Broadway attains to a nescience the magnitude and splendour of which dazzle and stagger. It is not meet to dismiss the phenomenon lightly, carelessly, as one might dismiss a small schoolboy who says that two and two make five. The sheer superlativeness of the New York first-night audience makes it an unmistakably important and valuable item for laboratory investigation. Just like sulphureted hydrogen.

# Chapter Thirteen: Its Typical Season

For the benefit of curious historians and statisticians of, let us say, one hundred years from now — and by way of placing on record a typical American theatrical year in the early period of the present, or twentieth, century — I propose herewith a literal and unadorned, if fragmentary, account of the events and philosophies theatrical of the season of 1916–1917 as those manifestations passed before the vision of one like myself, a professional playgoer. These records, as I say, I shall present in the main without criticism. I shall rather incline myself where possible to the other side and set briefly down precisely what were the gospel adventures of the eye and the ear in the popular theatres of New York City during the stipulated period. Whether or not my impressions and experiences were the typical and common experiences and impressions of the less regular playgoer, I leave to the latter: I believe they were. And I therefore make bold to hope that this fractional record may be, at some far distant and probably more cultured theatrical day, of some slight archeological interest and value.

### THE DIARY

*July 31, 1916.* To the Cort Theatre to see what was announced as a new and original farce-comedy by Mr. Edward Clark named "Coat-Tales." Arrived twenty minutes after the curtain had risen. Discovered a minute later that what I was seeing was the old and familiar Maupassant fur coat *conte* treated to a vaudeville technique. Departed.

*August 8, 1916.* To the George M. Cohan Theatre to see what was announced as a new and original comedy by Mr. Roi Cooper Megrue named "Seven Chances." At quarter of nine o'clock found I was watching the dramatization of a magazine story I had read several years before, a story that was, in turn, a revamping of Hoyt's "A Black Sheep" which I had seen when I was eight years old, and of divers stage distillations I had seen at the respective ages of ten, eleven, thirteen — I had the scarlet fever when twelve and was not taken to the theatre that year — fourteen, fifteen, eighteen — I was abroad at sixteen and seventeen,— nineteen and on to thirty-five.

*August 9, 1916.* To the Eltinge Theatre to see what was announced as a new and original play by Mr. Max Marcin called "Cheating Cheaters." Found at 9:22 P. M. that I was being made privy once again to the same general type of crook plot that had seen service in a play by Kate Jordan Vermilye called "Secret Strings," which I had seen several years before in the Longacre Theatre, at which latter in turn I had found at 9:18 P. M. that I was being made privy once again to the same general type of crook plot that had seen service in an O. Henry story called " Shearing the Wolf."

*August 10, 1916.* To the Longacre to see what was announced as a new and original play by Otto Hauerbach called " The Silent Witness." Found at 8 :34 that what I was about to behold was one of the annual unloosings of the old " Madame X " plot. Thereupon started reading Edmond de Goncourt's " La Fille Elise " and got to page 150 before the final curtain fell.

*August 14, 1916.* To the Lyceum to see " Please Help Emily," by H. M. Harwood, the typical British idea of Frenchy farce in which a bachelor, coming home late at night, finds a strange and very pretty girl in his bed and therefore spends the rest of the night at his club.

*August 15, 1916.* " Broadway and Buttermilk," Mr. Willard Mack, Maxine Elliott Theatre. A sentimental document, interspersed with ragtime lays, apotheosizing the superior virtues of the rural yokel. The author was seated in a stage box, chewing gum.

*August 16, 1916.* To see a mixed identity farce at the Republic named " His Bridal Night," in which the vaudeville Sisters Dolly played the leading rôles and in which the plot demanded that the main male mime be unable to distinguish one of the sisters, who resembles Gertrude Elliott at twenty-one, from the other sister, who resembles Madame Janauschek at thirty-four.

*August 17, 1916.* To the Astor to see what was

[171]

announced as a new and original play entitled " The Guilty Man," by Ruth Davis and Charles Klein. Found at 8:43 that I was beholding François Coppée's " L'Homme Culpable " and the only local revamping of the " Madame X " plot since the 10th inst. When Miss Fenwick was not on the stage, read into J. K. Huysmans' " Certains."

*August 18, 1916.* To the Gaiety to see " Turn to the Right," by the Messrs. Winchell Smith and John Hazzard, a play about the wayward son, the gray-haired mother, the mortgage on the old farm, the skinflint deacon and the real pump.

*August 21, 1916.* To the Shubert to see " The Happy Ending," by J. and L. Macpherson. An undergraduate Maeterlinckian brew on the merry quality of death. Heaven revealed as a platform covered with grass cloth, illuminated by two powerful white bunchlights, and peopled by some dozen or more exceedingly bad actors.

*August 22, 1916.* Thirty-ninth Street Theatre — a music show entitled " Yvette." Directly after the opening chorus at 8:25, the German dialect comedian came out, opened his coat, disclosed a loud red vest and addressed a remark to a fellow pantaloon who thereupon struck with his cane upon the comedian's right shin which had a small board attached to it underneath the trousers and so gave issue to a resounding crack. In bed at 8:47. My regularly assigned seat in this theatre, J 23, is adjacent to a draughty exit, the Shuberts thus evidently plotting toward my demise.

*August 26, 1916.* Thirty-ninth Street Theatre.

[172]

A British farce by W. W. Ellis called " A Little Bit of Fluff." A mid-Victorian version of " Please Help Emily," by a writer who imagined that his audience would laugh itself half to death when he caused one of his characters to peek through a keyhole and caused another quickly to pull open the door, thus causing the first character to sprawl on the floor. My seat still adjacent to the draughty exit, the Shuberts doubtless planning, by making these frequent changes of plays in this theatre, to bring about fatal symptoms with dispatch.

*August 28, 1916.* James T. Powers in " Somebody's Luggage," by Mark Swan, at the Forty-eighth Street Theatre. The kind of farce in which a man accidentally gets hold of another man's traveling bag and is therefore for the next three months mistaken for the latter by everyone including the butler who has been in the service of the real owner of the bag since childhood. Mr. Powers is the sort of comedian who believes that comedy consists chiefly in walking across the stage at frequent intervals in the manner of a man whose one leg is considerably shorter than the other.

*August 29, 1916.* To the Longacre to see what was announced as a new and original farce, by the Messrs. Brown, Lewis and Hauerbach, called " A Pair of Queens." Found at 8:45 that I was spectator at practically the same crook-detective farce I had seen in this same theatre the season before — then by Frederick Jackson and called " A Full House."

*August 30, 1916.* A music show in the Forty-fourth Street Theatre called "The Girl from Brazil." Chorus girls' average age, 18 years (B. C.).

*August 31, 1916.* To the Hippodrome. Excellent amusement for persons who estimate everything by size, and so regard Fatty Arbuckle's posterior as of vastly greater importance than Gerhart Hauptmann's brain.

*September, 1, 1916.* To the Globe Theatre to see a farce called "Fast and Grow Fat," by George Broadhurst — a farce every bit as full of laughter as "Rosmersholm." Read L. Lind-af-Hageby's biography of Strindberg and thereafter got as far as page 47 in Georges Pelissier's "Le Mouvement Littéraire Contemporain."

*September 2, 1916.* To the Playhouse. The play, "The Man Who Came Back." The author, Jules Eckert Goodman. The plot: A dissolute young man so insults a Barbary Coast cabaret singer by implying that she is not virtuous that the young woman becomes an opium fiend and an habituée of a notorious dive in Shanghai. She remains physically pure, however, and once again happening upon the dissolute young man in the dive, marries him and reforms him.

*September 4, 1916.* "The Flame," by Richard Walton Tully, Lyric Theatre. An inscrutable mixture of Central American politics, voodooism, obstetrics and cooch dancing. At 9:27 gave it up as a too difficult job and spent the balance of the evening in periodic discreet peekings over my shoulder at a great beauty enthroned behind me.

*September 11, 1916.* To the Casino to hear a

music show called " Flora Bella." Observed on the program that one of the characters was named Prince Demidoff. The allusion to the Prince as Prince Demi-tasse occurred somewhat later than usual, at 9:18. The libretto concerned a man who failed to recognize his wife at a masked ball, the wife being completely disguised by a two-inch mask worn over her eyes.

*September 12, 1916.* To Edward Knoblauch's " Paganini " at the Criterion, in which Mr. George Arliss succeeded brilliantly in depicting the great Paganini as Mr. George Arliss.

*September 14, 1916.* " Nothing But the Truth," by James Montgomery, at the Longacre. A new and original farce like " The Naked Truth," by George Paston, which was produced eight years before.

*September 19, 1916.* Eleanor H. Porter's " Pollyanna," dramatized by Catherine Chisholm Cushing, in the Hudson. Philosophy of the play: One should be happier when one breaks a leg than when one loses a dollar bill, for where the leg will surely, in time, get well again, one may never recover the dollar bill. Read Dostoievski's " Crime and Punishment."

*September 20, 1916.* W. Somerset Maugham's " Caroline " at the Empire. Oscar Wilde died November 30, 1900. *Verbis meis addere nihil audebant et super illos stillabat eloquium meum.— Job xxix, 22. R. I. P.*

*September 21, 1916.* To the Globe to hear a music show named " The Amber Empress." The libretto of the fortune-hunting Count, the climbing American mother, the saucer-eyed daughter in the pink dress and carrying the pale blue parasol, the noble young American in the Norfolk jacket and sport shirt, and the final unmasking of the villaino. Music of the bass drum and sandpaper school.

*September 25, 1916.* " Miss Springtime," music show, New Amsterdam Theatre. Mr. Abraham Erlanger, the manager of this theatre, believes Hall Caine to be the greatest of living literary artists and his play, " Margaret Schiller," one of the really great dramatic compositions of the present time. I don't. Mr. Abraham Erlanger has accordingly punished my insularity by depriving me of my seat in his theatre. I did not, therefore, see " Miss Springtime."

*September 26, 1916.* Cyril Harcourt's " The Intruder," Cohan and Harris Theatre. Wife, husband, lover. Husband finds out. Alarums and excursions. Husband forgives wife.

*September 27, 1916.* To see the Hattons' " Upstairs and Down." Saw Hermann Bahr's " Principle " metamorphosed into a so-called snappy story — a fable of baccarat, bacardi and bordello — Long Island smart society as seen from the vantage point of Long Beach.

*September 28, 1916.* To the Fulton. " Over Night," etc., etc., with the back drop painted up to represent a Belgian village instead of the usual inn up the Hudson. This time called " Arms and the Girl."

*October 2, 1916.* To the Thirty-ninth Street

Theatre. "Backfire," a Charles Klein opus by Stuart Olivier, in which the blonde stenographer turns the tables, as usual, on the millionaire who ruined her papa. The Shuberts still assigning me to the seat next to the draughty exit. Their subtle plot succeeding. I catch a chill.

*October 3, 1916.* "Hush," an English importation, at the Little Theatre. An attempt to shock the yokelry by causing a young unmarried girl to talk about having a baby — it subsequently developing that the young unmarried girl who talks about having a baby has written a play about a young married girl who has a baby, to which young married girl's baby the young unmarried girl has all the while really been alluding.

*October 4, 1916.* To the Maxine Elliott to see William Hodge's "Fixing Sister." Here, the libretto of "The Amber Empress" presented without chorus girls and ragtime tunes and palmed off as "an American comedy." The Duke unmasked and in bad at 10:40. I undressed and in bed at 9:40.

*October 5, 1916.* To the Forty-eighth Street Theatre to see George Broadhurst's "Rich Man, Poor Man," still another conscription of the Cinderella story. In bed at 10:02 P. M.

*October 6, 1916.* Harris Theatre. A hokum version of Galsworthy's "Justice" by the Messrs. Megrue and Cobb, in the last act of which Mr. George Nash and the Lee Lash scenic artist reform a prison.

*October 11, 1916.* To the Garrick to "Le Poilu," a patriotic French music show in the French tongue, financed by the French Otto Kahn and Lee Shubert, with music by the French Sigmund Romberg sung by the French Belle Ashlyn, Pearl Glover and Zelda Johnstone, with dances staged by the French Jack Mason, and scenery painted by the French August Blumendorf.

*October 14, 1916.* To the motion picture "Intolerance" at the Liberty. This picture, widely announced as the cinema's *chef-d'œuvre,* consisted largely, during the time I remained in the theatre, of showings upon the screen of cuties and quotations from the Encyclopedia Britannica. I entertain no personal, or critical, objection to either cuties or the Encyclopedia Britannica. But I don't fancy them together.

*October 23, 1916.* To the George M. Cohan Theatre to see "She Stoops to Conquer" in sub-Mason and Dixon dialect. Title, "Come Out of the Kitchen." The Goldsmith, Mr. A. E. Thomas.

*October 28, 1916.* To the Criterion to view Mr. John Drew in sideburns entitled "Major Pendennis." Author of the sideburns, Mr. Langdon Mitchell. Inspiration of the sideburns, the Thackeray novel.

*October 30, 1916.* Empire Theatre. Scene: "A hall in Cheviot Castle, Northumberland. Night." The hero overhears the whispered conversation of the villain and Mrs. Radford and thwarts their plot. Scene: "The same. Thirty-eight hours later. Early afternoon." The hero marries Diana, the erstwhile fiancée of the villain, whom he

[178]

has loved from that day — you remember, sweetheart — the sky was blue and the birds, etc., etc. Title, "The Basker." Author, Clifford Mills.

*October 31, 1916.* To Clare Kummer's "Good Gracious Annabelle" in the Republic Theatre. A civilized farce and an amusing evening.

*November 2, 1916.* "Old Lady 31," a delightful sentimental comedy of old age by Rachel Crothers and Louise Forsslund. Thirty-ninth Street Theatre. The Shuberts still assigning me to the seat adjoining the draughty exit. Their plot making excellent headway. I get an attack of tonsilitis.

*November 6, 1916.* To the Booth to see a performance of Shaw's "Getting Married," a play to be acted in the theatre in the same sense that Mrs. Rorer's Cook Book is a book to be read in the library.

*November 13, 1916.* To the Washington Square Players' new bill of one-act plays, not one of which showed an artist going to sleep and dreaming that his painting of a beautiful girl had come to life.

*November 14, 1916.* To see Rida Johnson Young's farce, "Captain Kidd, Jr.," a Christian Science version of "Treasure Island." The central comic figure of the manuscript, a country constable who periodically flicked up the bottom of his vest and disclosed his badge of office secreted on his abdomen.

*November 15, 1916.* To the Neighbourhood Playhouse to see a bill of Shaw and Dunsany short plays. A genuinely satisfying evening. My companion, Mr. Robert H. Davis, forced to admit that Shaw is almost as amusing as Irvin Cobb.

[179]

*November 18, 1916.* To the Harris Theatre to see Margaret Illington in the leading rôle of Hopwood's deft naughty farce, " Our Little Wife," which the majority of my colleagues condemned on the moral ground that only young girls weighing under one hundred and two pounds should be cast for objectionable rôles.

*November 25, 1916.* A woman writes a sensationally successful novel. *She keeps the news from her husband!* Title, " Such Is Life." Princess Theatre.

*November 27, 1916.* To view J. Hartley Manners' drama, " The Harp of Life." Theme: A young man's mother desires above all things that her son shall grow up to respect all women. The young man falls deeply in love with a woman and plans to make her his wife. His mother reveals to the young man the fact that the woman he loves is a common prostitute. The young man therefore grows up to respect all women.

*November 28, 1916.* A good-for-nothing young city fellow goes to the country. He meets a country girl. She reforms him. He invents a machine which he sells to the Trust for $500,000 and they live happily ever afterward. Title, " Mile-a-Minute Kendall." Creator, Owen Davis. Place, Lyceum Theatre.

*November 29, 1916.* To a Casino music show called " Follow Me." At 9:02 P. M. Miss Anna Held came out and proceeded to confide to the audience that her eyes were of an exceptionally passionate quality. Inasmuch as I had been privileged the

[180]

same confidence by the lady back in Evans and Hoey's "Parlor Match" in 1898 or thereabout, I failed to consider the confession news and went across the street to the Opera House.

*December 4, 1916.* To the Empire to see Sarah Bernhardt. Rosemary in mothballs. . . . Love letters in the hands of the prosecuting attorney. . . . "Auld Lang Syne" by a Jazz band at 3 A. M. . . . Grandmother reading an Elsie book.

*December 5, 1916.* To the Fulton to see Arnold Daly in Bahr's "The Master." A good play well acted.

*December 6, 1916.* To the Astor to see a music show named "Her Soldier Boy." Plot of book: He wasn't killed after all, but only wounded. Plot of jokes: "As you say in America, bah Jove, 'I've got your numeral!'"

*December 7, 1916.* A middle-aged man falls in love with his ward. He hesitates to declare his passion. He declares his passion. The ward says she has loved him all the time. Title, "Margery Daw." Author, George Parker. Place, Princess Theatre.

*December 22, 1916.* To Mr. Belasco's theatre to see "Little Lady in Blue," a conventional vehicle for a star actress possessed of all the conventional component parts of such a vehicle save wheels. Thesis: Wayward fellow, sweet soubrette, reform and matrimony.

*December 25, 1916.* To the Empire to view Barrie's "A Kiss for Cinderella," regarding which my confrère, M. Clayton Hamilton, his nose a deep

[181]

maroon from unrestrained weeping, piped this affecting *chanson:*

"If millions and millions of lilies-of-the-valley were miraculously turned to silver and simultaneously shaken, there would arise a light and laughing music in the world — a music so delicate that it would be inaudible to ears that cannot hear. First of all, the infant children, too soft as yet to sit up and take notice of anything but light and sound, would turn their tiny heads upon their necks and smile as if in memory of a noble thought, heard somewhere long ago. Next, the Little People, whose other name is Fairies and who live forever in the minds of those who cannot quite forget, would troop out under leaves and petals, and join their hands and dance around in rings. And high, high up beyond the treetops, the ever-circling stars would sing as once they sang upon the primal morning, ere yet the universe grew old. And everywhere beneath the circling and the singing of the stars, the Tall People, whose other name is Poets, would listen and would softly smile and exquisitely weep. If you have tears, by all means go and shed them as a sort of exquisite libation to the latest masterpiece of Sir James Matthew Barrie, Baronet (for services to humankind); but, if you have not tears, by all means stay away and make room for the rest of us who want to blow a kiss to Cinderella."

Since the play seems to the present somewhat less impressionable writer to be a work considerably inferior to Miss Eleanor Gates' "Poor Little Rich Girl," and more greatly inferior still to Barrie's previous plays, he has decided to stay away, as requested, and allow the moist M. Hamilton this extra room wherein to blow kisses.

*December 26, 1916.* To the Hudson. "The

Lion and the Mouse," Vol. II, No. 136. Title, " Shirley Kaye." Rewriter, Hulbert Footner.

*December 27, 1916.* To Stuart Walker's Portmanteau Theatre and the admirable plays of Dunsany. The finest things of the season. An evening to the taste of such persons as fail to enthuse over dramas in which an old negro woman goes crazy because her newly born niece is disclosed to have a taint of white blood.

*January 1, 1917, matinée.* At the Maxine Elliott a play by Mrs. May Martindale called " Gamblers All," an echo of such *contes* of the yesteryear as " A Woman's Atonement, or A Mother's Mistake," by Adah M. Howard, and " Leslie's Loyalty, or His Love So True," by Charles Garvice.

*January 1, 1917, evening.* To the Criterion to see " Seremonda," by William Lindsey, a romantic drama of the species in which the barbaric Raimon, waving aside Barral, Amfos, Timon, Ugo, Ermengarda, Vidal and Gondolfo, runs the lover Guilhem through the gizzard with his trusty blade and grasps the coveted and swooning Julia Arthur to his brawny bosom.

*January 6, 1917.* To the Maxine Elliott to see " The Lodger," the play in which the timid and very gentle comedian is mistaken for a bloodthirsty criminal. Mimeographer, Horace Vachell.

*January 8, 1917.* To the Lyceum to see a revival of A. E. Thomas' " Her Husband's Wife," a tenuous but adroit comedy in which, on this occasion, the comedy rested chiefly in the spectacle of Mr. Henry Kolker playing a modish beau in a pair of trousers that would have been two feet too long for De Wolf Hopper.

*January 10, 1917.* Princess Theatre. " 'Ception Shoals," by H. Austin Adams, the play about the young girl who is brought up on the isolated island, believes that babies are the result of shaking hands a'd then, on her eighteenth birthday, meets the leading man in the shirt open at the neck.

*January 11, 1917.* Fulton Theatre. " In for the Night," by James Savery, the farce about the couple who are mistaken by the hotel clerk for man and wife and assigned to the same bedroom as the curtain falls on the second act, the curtain rising on the third act (time: next morning) and disclosing the man asleep in the armchair downstairs.

*January 15, 1917.* To a music show hight " Love o' Mike," Shubert Theatre. The kind of entertainment presented annually by the University of Missoula Falseface Club. A so-called smart air imparted to the proceedings through periodic ejaculations of such phrases as " top hole " and " bally bounder."

*February 1, 1917.* To see what was announced as an inspiring Biblical play in the Manhattan Opera House. Title, " The Wanderer." Plot: A bad boy leaves his home in ancient Hebron in order to see the Russian Ballet which is showing in Babylon. At the performance he falls for a cocotte who robs him and then throws him over for a sailor. He returns to his home town and marries his country girl sweetheart.

*February 5, 1917.* To the Booth to view Clare

Kummer's " A Successful Calamity." Plot: A rich man, whose wife drags him nightly to ulterior functions, longs to spend one quiet evening at home. To this end, he tells his wife he has lost all his money. His longing to enjoy a quiet evening at home thereupon at length vouchsafed him, he discovers that the end of the first act needs an effective " curtain " and promptly goes off to a prize-fight. But a beautifully produced and excellently acted play.

*February 6, 1917.* To Miss Jane Cowl's " Lilac Time," the kind of war play in which all the soldiers have their hair slicked down with pomade and in which the poor French peasant girl has her mouth rouged into a little Cupid's bow.

*February 7, 1917.* An old California gentleman goes to sleep. He dreams that his Japanese butler, accompanied by the Japanese butlers of three of his neighbours, invades unsuspecting America and captures the whole Pacific coast. He wakes up and calls on the audience to accept his vision as a warning. Title, " If." Creative Brain, Mr. Mark Swan.

*February 9, 1917.* To the Morosco Theatre to see " Canary Cottage," the kind of music show in which a comedian named Asbestos Hicks explains that his parents named him Asbestos because he was such a warm baby.

*February 10, 1917.* Little Theatre. " The Morris Dance." 8:30 P. M., Mr. Winthrop Ames believes Granville Barker to be a great man. 8:50 P. M., a misgiving seizes Mr. Ames. 9:20 P. M., Mr. Ames calls for spirits of ammonia. 9:36 P. M.,

[185]

Mr. Ames observed in lobby passing Mr. Barker without bowing.

*February 12, 1917.* To the Maxine Elliott to see Chesterton's charming and unusual play, " Magic," sadly filtered through a 182-pound Patricia, a Stranger with a voice like the late Ezra Kendall's, and a misty plantation that took a period of time ample for the leisurely palating of five beers at the Kaiserhof bar next door wherein to fade into the drawing-room of the Duke.

*February 13, 1917.* Criterion Theatre. The unpolished American with the heart of gold unmasks the Duke who is wooing the young heiress and marries the latter. Title, " Johnny Get Your Gun." Cerebrum, E. L. Burke.

*February 14, 1917.* To the Washington Square Players' new program of one-act plays. A but moderately interesting bill marred by Maeterlinck's wearying asthma, "The Death of Tintagiles." Still no sign of a one-act play dealing with an actress who, while waiting for her train at a jerk-water junction, patches up a quarrel between a stage-struck country lass and her farmer-boy lover.

*February 19, 1917.* To the Princess to see the Bolton-Wodehouse music show " Oh Boy." *Two* pretty girls. Therefore exceptionally good entertainment.

*February 26, 1917.* Fulton Theatre. Damon and Pythias in hobo make-up. Much fervent hand-shaking, old-man-ing, God-bless-you-Jack-ing, slapping-on-the-back, etc. Title, " Pals First."

*February 27, 1917.* To see a revival of Barrie's

originally warming " Professor's Love Story." Like reading a woman's love letters fifteen years after you've married her.

*March 5, 1917.* To the Garrick to see E. H. Sothern's play " Stranger Than Fiction." Mr. Sothern's idea of satire provides an admirable satire of Mr. Sothern. Home and in bed before the entr'acte orchestra had got to Dvôrák's " Humoréske."

*March 6, 1917.* To " The Willow Tree," by Rhodes and Benrimo. " Madam Butterfly " on a xylophone. . . . Reading aloud the fable of Galatea in Vantine's. . . . Moonlight on a dish of chop suey.

*March 7, 1917.* To the Harris to see a play called " The Brat." A street urchin is brought into the home of a well-to-do family, captures the household with her great wit, reforms the dissolute son of the house and marries him. Author, Maude Fulton.

*March 12, 1917.* To Somerset Maugham's " Our Betters," at the Hudson. Wedekind with a monocle. . . . A young girl reading the *Police Gazette* hidden between the covers of *Town Topics.* . . . The ghost of Clyde Fitch having tea with the ghost of Josie Mansfield.

*March 19, 1917.* To the Thirty-ninth Street Theatre to see Galsworthy's " The Fugitive," an 1895 triangle play into which Galsworthy has inserted a couple of speeches on the British divorce laws of 1915 and so persuaded most of the New York reviewers that his play is " a vigorous, up-to-the-moment indictment of the inequality of a wife's position in the English divorce courts." The Shuberts still placing me next to the draughty exit in Row J, and their plot against me getting on famously. I catch the lumbago and have to see a doctor.

*March 20, 1917.* To hear the musical comedy "Eileen," in which Victor Herbert shows Reginald DeKoven how he should have written "The Highwayman."

*March 22, 1917.* To the Bandbox to see the Urban-Ordynski futurist production of Ossip Dymov's play "Nju." Galsworthy's "Fugitive" in motion-picture scenario form, with scenery and lighting effects by the President of Liberia.

*March 26, 1917.* To the Lyceum to see Vachell's "Case of Lady Camber," the play about the phial of poison, the suspicion attaching to the pretty nurse, the examination of the phial, the finding that the cork has not been pulled and the exoneration of the Nightingale. See "Audrey's Recompense, or How Her Honour Was Spared," by Mrs. Georgie Sheldon and "Her Fatal Move, or Cleared at Last," by Mrs. Alex. McVeigh Miller.

*March 28, 1917.* To the new one-act plays of the Washington Square Players. Not one of the one-act plays, alas, contained the fine dramatic situation of the husband who returns unexpectedly and finds his wife in her lover's arms, only to be disarmed by the assurance of the latter, a playwright, that the wife and he were merely rehearsing a scene from his new play.

[188]

*April 7, 1917.* To the Garrick to a play called " Grasshopper." A play of German peasant life adapted into a play of Irish peasant life. Chauncey Olcott in " The Weavers." . . . Emanuel Reicher in " The Heart of Paddy Whack." Original author, von Keyserling.

*April 9, 1917.* The several friends of a young man given to excessive bibbing try to prove to him that his indulgence in alcohol is ruining his mind, his health and his career. The young man, in turn, disproves each and every one of their arguments. In view of which, and by virtue of the further fact that the young man's robust father who has never touched a drink in his life falls dead at the mere spectacle of the young man drinking a small pony of brandy, the play is called a strong argument in favour of prohibition. Title of play, " The Very Minute." The Brieux of the occasion, Mr. John Meehan. Place, Belasco Theatre.

*April 10, 1917.* To the New Amsterdam, by special dispensation, to hear the talented Max Beerbohm's lesser brother Herbert's most recent curtain speech assuring Americans how much he loves them (at $2.50 a head) and his enactment, *en passant,* of a Michael Morton version of " The Newcomes." Thackeray in terms of the Union Dime Savings Bank.

*April 12, 1917.* A pure Southern girl is abducted and deflowered by a white slaver. Her fiancé, a physician, catches the white slaver after prowling around a dark stage for fifteen minutes with a pocket flashlight and shouts that he will avenge his beloved's honour by inoculating the white slaver with various experimental toxins. Title, " The Knife." Author, Eugene Walter. Place, Bijou Theatre.

*April 13, 1917.* To the Provincetown Players' one-act plays. Wit in place of the comique with the target sewed to the seat of his trousers, and an observation of life in place of the usual observation of the predilections and tastes of vaudeville audiences.

*April 14, 1917.* To Ridgely Torrence's negro plays at the Garden Theatre. Padraic Colum in black face. An interesting beginning, at least.

*April 18, 1917.* Republic Theatre. A dramatization of Du Maurier's " Peter Ibbetson," with recalcitrant trick scenery and a 200-pound little Mimsey interposed between the manuscript and the imagination. My confrère Hamilton, deeply touched, again composes a *chanson* on lilies of the valley, soft little babies, dancing dandelions and laughing little stars.

*April 23, 1917.* Went to the Forty-fourth Street Theatre and watched Mr. Robert B. Mantell give his celebrated performance of the rôle of Macbeth in his presentation of Shakespeare's " Merchant of Venice."

*April 27, 1917.* To the " Midnight Frolic " on the New Amsterdam Theatre roof. I drank two cocktails, three glasses of sherry, a quart of champagne and several ponies of Cointreau. The show seemed to get better and better as it went along.

*April 30, 1917.* To the Astor to see a music

show called " His Little Widows," the plot of which requests one to imagine that all the girls on the stage are wild to marry Mr. Carter De Haven.

*May 14, 1917.* To the Empire to see three one-act plays by J. M. Barrie. The first, " The New Word," the war in terms of Barrie. The second, " Old Friends," dipsomania in terms of Macdonald Hastings. The third, " The Old Lady Shows Her Medals," the war in terms of Gertrude Jennings.

*May 15, 1917.* To the Glen Springs Sanatorium.

# Chapter Fourteen: Its "Big Time" Vaudeville

Vaudeville may be described as a form of theatrical entertainment devised for the delectation of admirers of green plush Alpine hats, detective stories in which it is finally revealed that the man was murdered by an East Indian chimpanzee belonging to the Mahatma from the eye of whose idol the sacred rhinestone had been pilfered, scarf-pins in the form of question marks, reproductions of paintings showing a man kneeling tenderly beside an ornate bed and kissing the hand of his wife who has recently vouchsafed him a baby, and reversible undershirts. It is made up, for the most part, of young men whose coat-pockets are cut on a slant of ninety degrees and embellished with flaps fashioned in the shape of W's, and of young women whose speaking voices resemble that of Galli-Curci's cab-starter. It is the profession of these young women to rush out onto the stage carrying suit-cases, bump violently into the aforementioned young men and ejaculate " Mon Doo! Quelque chose est ici," and the profession of the young men thereupon to observe " Ah, a native of Passaic! "

In addition to these young men and women, vaudeville contains all the old actors in the world who are out of work and whose specialty on the so-called legitimate stage was playing the rôle of the police captain, to say nothing of all the vintage coloratura sopranos who have had fights with Mr. Charles Dillingham and the Shuberts because the latter assigned them to dressing-rooms one flight up. Each of the old police captain actors appears in a sketch in which his burglar son breaks by night into an apartment not knowing that the apartment is that of his own father, and each of the vintage coloraturas winds up on the last note of all her songs by shaking herself like a wet dog and suddenly throwing open her arms like the angel on the wire in the " Uncle Tom's Cabin " transformation scene.

Besides the sketch in which the police captain actors appear, a great favourite in vaudeville is the sketch in which the wife pleads with her husband to give up something or other since, in the months he has been away, a condition has arisen that will shortly make him a father. Another sketch close to the hearts of vaudeville audiences is the one played in front of a back-drop on which are painted two cherry trees in bloom and the peak of Fujiyama. In this sketch, some Broadway ingénue out of a job appears as the young daughter of a Japanese nobleman. The young daughter, so goes the sketch, has been educated at Eton and upon returning to her native Yokohama is followed by young Roderick Trevor who loves her madly and who has come hither to ask her father for her hand in marriage. Pink Arbutus, as the daughter is called, breaks the news to her honourable father in the honourable garden of their honourable pagoda. Her stoical father refuses his consent and tells Pink Arbutus a fable in which is recounted the fate of poor little Princess Chu Chu Karr who, too, unwisely loved a foreigner. After Pink Arbutus' father leaves, Roderick vaults over the garden wall and breathes his love into little Pink Arbutus' ear. As the sweet amour is in progress, a couple of Pink Arbutus' father's myrmidons goose-step up behind Roderick, pinion his arms behind him and, despite little Pink Arbutus' ululations, carry him into the pagoda.

Enters now again the father who is determined to press Pink Arbutus to his stern will. But no sooner has he seized the little one's wrists than rushes on Roderick's mother, who has followed her son to Japan on the same mail packet.

" Pray God, I am not too late ! " she cries.

" For what, honourable English lady ? " bids Pink Arbutus *père,* in an O'Sullivan rubber heel voice.

" To prevent my son's union with an Oriental ! " she sneers.

This remark makes Pink Arbutus *père* jolly good and sore. But the dénouement comes when, moved to compassion, he confesses that Pink Arbutus is not of his own flesh and blood, but merely his adopted child, her parents, none· other than Lord and Lady Spencer Warwick, having been slain in the Boxer rebellion.

Still another greatly admired sketch may be described thus :

# ITS VAUDEVILLE

SCENE: *The home of John D. Morgan,*
*a millionaire.*

9 P. M.— Curtain rises disclosing a **room** with green
walls, purple velvet portières, red upholstered
chairs, a bird's-eye maple piano, and a gilt centre
table with a small orange-shaded lamp.

9:01 P. M.—— Enter burglar who stealthily turns out
the light in the small lamp and then prowls around
with a pocket flash that makes twice as much light.

9:03 P. M.— Loud footsteps heard. Burglar hides
in closet at L 2. The small lamp is flashed on
and audience sees another burglar who then again
cautiously turns out the lamp and prowls around
with a doubly powerful pocket flashlight.

9:05 P. M.— Noise heard at window. Burglar hides
in closet at R 2. The small lamp is flashed on
and the audience sees another burglar who warily
turns out the lamp once again and prowls around
with an almost blinding pocket flashlight.

9:08 P. M.—— Sound of someone coming. Burglar
hides under table C. The small lamp is flashed
on and audience sees a girl in a salmon·pink dress
and pale blue stockings and slippers who turns
out the lamp and presently screams. The audience hears sounds of a gigantic struggle on the
darkened stage.

:12 P. M.—— Sound of the door being battered in.

[195]

Also, though there was no glass in the door, a great noise of shattered glass.

9:13 P. M.— The small lamp is turned up again.

9:13½ P. M.— The audience beholds two policemen covering the three burglars with revolvers while the girl stands crouched beside the piano.

9:14 P. M.— The first burglar pulls off his cap, announces that he is none other than Dick Maynard, of the United States Secret Service, and that he came to Morgan's house to trap the girl who, though posing as a member of the Morgan household, is in reality Red Nellie, the Harlem safe-cracker.

9:15 P. M.— The second burglar pulls off his cap, announces that he is none other than Bob Blaisdell, of the United States Secret Service, and that he came to trap the first secret service agent who was suspected by the Chief of being crooked.

9:16 P. M.— The third burglar pulls off his cap, announces that he is none other than John D. Morgan himself and that he came to trap the second secret service agent who is in reality a confederate of Red Nellie.

9:17 P. M.— Red Nellie pulls off her wig, announces that she is none other than Sally O'Brien, a private detective, and that she came to trap Morgan who was suspected of attempting to rob his own house.

9:18 P. M.— The two policemen pull off their false beards, announce that they are, respectively, John D. Morgan and his son, John D. Morgan, Jr., and that they now at length have the four notorious crooks — the three men and the woman — cornered!

9:18½ P. M.— The stage-hand pulls down the curtain.

9:18¾ P. M.— The audience pulls off the wrappers of its Tutti-Frutti and gets ready for the classic dancers.

Probably the finest thing in vaudeville, however, is the act showing the reunion of the old Union and the old Confederate soldier who celebrate the *entente cordiale* by jointly executing a soft shoe dance interspersed with somersaults and thereafter playing a medley of " Dixie " and " Marching Through Georgia " on cornets, though there are connoisseurs who prefer the gentleman in the blue dress suit who sings the song about following a girl for nine blocks only to find it was a Scotchman in kilts. There is a difference of opinion about vaudeville, as with everything else. Where some can barely keep from laughing themselves off their seats and tumbling into the aisle in a ready-to-burst paroxysm when the comique in the wide red pants steps into the footlight trough and alludes to it as the Subway, others who get merely a side-ache laughing at the comique simply can't control themselves and get completely doubled up when the man in the purple coat with the belt at the back says to the man in the green coat with the belt at the back, " You know my girl? Her name is Plaster. I go to court Plaster every night. She is a poor girl but there's lots of other girls as por-ous Plaster."

But, granting to vaudeville these substantial virtues, it yet seems to me that there is something lacking. This lack, I daresay, lies in the more recent refinement of vaudeville — a refinement that must already have unmistakably impressed itself upon the reader — and the consequent passing from vaudeville of its quondam irresistible slapstick tonics. In place of the good old days when the little green-whiskered Irishman fell onto the stage backwards through the swinging door and, colliding with the fat blonde in the red satin *décolleté,* caused the latter to land upon his stomach with a resounding kerplunk, present-day vaudeville presents us with an aloof and tony society atmosphere in which the mauve dress coats of the gentlemen fasten in front with a loop, in which the ladies in golf clothes carry lorgnettes and in which the butlers in the dramatic sketches are dressed up to look like Thomas Jefferson at an important State dinner. As vaudeville has acquired this air of elegance, this atmosphere of smartness, this *recherché* quality, there has coincidentally departed from it its old bounce and gusto. Gone that palmy and inspiriting day when the sensitive, artistic

Sister Act in short green skirts with red linings
meandered out before the drop-curtain embellished
with Beeman's bald head and hook-and-eye and root
beer ads., nonchalantly scrutinized the dressy old
boy in the stage box who had sneaked away from
the office to take in the matinée, and then went at
"My Gal's a Highborn Lady" like twin gold-
toothed contralto siege guns. Gone, too, the lady
in the white satin Mother Hubbard who sat in the
spotlight and played sad stuff on a harp, withdrawing
her hand in magnificent gesture after each pluck,
and meanwhile chewing a greak hunk of gum. And
gone with these, alas, the old slappings in the face
with the *Police Gazette,* the old wipings of the saliva
out of the eye upon the Dutch comedian's pronuncia-
tion of any word containing more than one S, the
old cloutings over the ear with the stuffed rolling-pin,
the lusty old fetches upon the trousers' seat with the
slapstick containing the blank cartridge.

Those, gentlemen, were the high days of vaudeville! Those the days before vaudevillians became
educated and polished, as we find them today, and
before they learned to say "I seen" instead of "I
have saw." Those the days when someone's hand
got stuck in the neck of a decanter at least four times
on every bill and when the mind-readers, instead of
having confederates in the downstairs audience, simply rattled off answers to imaginary questions by persons seated (if one followed the eyes of the blind-
folded mind-reader's husband) somewhere in the
air between the balcony and the gallery. Well, well,
I seem to grow sentimental! But the scent of the

rosemary lingers in my nostrils and the memories of that lovely day will not be dimmed. Vaudeville, as we currently get it, fails equally to fill the heart and charm the senses.

The nature of this new vaudeville may be further established by an examination into what are called one-act war plays. These one-act war plays, if one may judge from a survey of the vaudeville stage during the past two years, fall into three specific groups. In the first group, we find the war plays in which a Broadway star in a loose brown dress and with a lot of chalk on her face has been violated by a drunken Prussian general, makes a long speech and then shoots herself rather than give birth to a Hun. In the second group, the war plays in which every suspicious person in the cast, with the exception of the overly curious and periodically visible stagehand who interprets the rôle of the enemy bombardment, turns out to be a member of the United States Secret Service. And in the third group, the war plays in which the French father kills his little Fifi rather than have her fall into the hands of the German barbarians and in which the vision of an actor dressed up to look unlike Lincoln is beheld through the gauze back-drop just as the curtain comes down.[1]

[1] *Nothing is so immediately inimical to the powers of imagination as colossal grandeur or stupendous tragedy. Imagination is not the sudden flower of great emotions born of great adventures and wondrous spectacles, but the meditative flower of what is intrinsically rather trivial. No man ever imagined a great poem while his eyes swept the vast magnificence of a Grand Canyon or the Inn Valley from a Hungerberg at Innsbruck. But more than one man has imagined a fine poem, and has written a fine poem, while his ardent*

# ITS VAUDEVILLE

The enormous acclaim with which these one-act war plays are received in modern big-time vaudeville is equalled only by the favour attending the one-act plays, or sketches, in which, respectively, the new doctor is mistaken for the gas-man, in which the baggage man who comes in to remove the trunks is mistaken for an English lord, in which the new maid is mistaken by the master of the house for his sister whom he hasn't seen for two years, in which the piano mover is mistaken by the young society girl for her millionaire fiancé, in which the new janitor is mistaken by the butler for his mistress' rich uncle from Brazil, in which an Irishwoman is mistaken by her husband for a fiery Spanish señorita with whom

*eyes swept the pulchritude of some dubious Helen or while along a country road his gaze rested on a violet. Thus, a great and dazzling canvas of war — such a war as that now raging in the world — blinds imagination rather than stimulates it. Itself greater than imagination, it dwarfs imagination into nothingness. Years must elapse, and perspective intervene, before it may give birth to a great novel, a great poem, a great drama.*

*Nowhere is this seeming paradox exhibited more clearly than in the theatre. One peace-time mother's grief gives theme-being to a Synge's rare imagination in terms of a "Riders to the Sea." A hundred housand wartime mothers' grief gives theme-being to nothing save tin-pot melodrama like "Seven Days' Leave" or "The White Feather." From the comparatively trivial springs a work of imaginative beauty; from the colossal springs a mere clattering of hollow cocoanut shells, firing of cap pistols and bombarding of papier-maché gunboats. A man writes a fine play about the last will and testament of a yokel (Pinero's "Thunderbolt"); another man writes a fine play about a fellow with a big nose (Rostand's "Cyrano de Bergerac"); still another writes a fine play about a woman with a mean disposition (Strindberg's "Father") — but a great war that shakes the world and its soul moves the man who beholds it and is shaken by it to the composition of the rankest sort of pot-boiler.*

he carried on at the masquerade ball the night before, in which the new chauffeur is mistaken for a paper hanger, and in which the new iceman is mistaken by the maid for the fashionable clubman expected for the reception. Slightly, though very slightly, less favoured are the kind of one-act plays in which, in a scene called " The Street of the Thousand Misdemeanors," a couple of characters named Virtue and Innocence swat a character named Temptation over the head with a club on which is painted the word Determination, to say nothing of the kind of one-act plays in which, when the curtain falls, a bachelor is sitting back in a chair listening to the daughter of his deceased sweetheart playing the old song on the piano.

As I have said, art may be art, but somehow I don't seem to care for this new classic vaudeville. I'd give it all, bag and baggage, for just five minutes once again with the homespun vaudeville show of twenty-five years ago, the vaudeville show in which the magnificently clad sidewalk conversationalist removed his high silk hat and placed it on the floor, and in which his disreputable hobo *confrère,* always mistaking the hat for a cuspidor, would then project thereinto an homeric and bewildering spit.

# Chapter Fifteen: Its "Small Time" Vaudeville

It is the secret ambition of all small boys around the age of seven to grow up to be the august personage in the blue shirt and embroidered galluses who stands with enviable hauteur on the back step of the ice-wagon and whose profession it is to hang the cake on the pendant brass dingus and determine that it is exactly the right amount under weight. It is the expressed ambition of all big artists of the so-called Small Time vaudeville around the ages of seventeen to seventy inclusive to grow up to be the august personage in the blue evening clothes and yellow chamois gloves who stands with modish disdain in the footlight trough of the Big Time Broadway vaudeville theatre and whose profession it is to ask the audience why the Kaiser was born in Bermuda and then quickly say it was because the Kaiser is a big onion.

The naïveté of these pickle herrings of the vaudeville preparatory school has about it not a little of the wistful and charming. Like so many artless Peter Pans they pursue through travail and hardship, over the rough road of the years, the rainbow at whose coveted end they may find the right sort of pancake derby and bunch of chin whiskers and heliotrope waistcoat wherewith to brew the necessary chuckle in the palates of the high priests, and so insure to themselves a hearing in some great vaudeville university on Broadway where tread the boards such baronial professors and *professorinen* of the art as Mademoiselle Tanguay, Mons. Houdini and Berkowitz's Trained Dogs. To the end that ultimately they may achieve this magnificent goal and attain to this proud estate, the souls of the Small Time strive and struggle tirelessly, tenaciously — and so great and obvious is this striving and struggle that the charitable heart must truly ache just a little when one of them like a certain Mr. Larry Comer, for example, after struggling for years to reach even the half-way goal of a Small Time stage in New York City and billing himself shrinkingly as " The Beau Brummel of Vaudeville," finds on the opening night of his appearance in Loew's theatre in West Forty-second Street that the vile ignoramus who printed the program had turned the " u " of the second word upside down and so announced Mr. Comer as " The Bean Brummel of Vaudeville."

Acquainted with, and appreciative of, such ribald catastrophes, one can not but be duly sympathetic toward such artists and artistes as take no chances and quite frankly and honestly, at space rates, announce their virtues to the world through the gazettes of their professions. Lying before me on my writing table is the copy of such a gazette (*Variety*) and I cull therefrom such confessionals as, for instance, that of a Mr. Johnny Dooley, who takes a half page advertisement modestly to announce that he is

1. The Most Versatile Comedian of the Day.
2. An Educated Gentleman.
3. An Artistic Character Actor.
4. A Trained Athlete.
5. A Clown, An Acrobat, A Musician. Can deliver a roaring comic song or a sympathetic ballad with equal success.
6. An Author.
7. An Originator with Up-to-the-Minute Ideas.

And as, for example, that of his partner, a Miss Yvette Rugel, who, getting in on the same advertisement, proclaims herself:

(1) A Beautiful, Refined, Wonderfully Formed Girl;
(2) A Remarkably Beautiful Cultivated Soprano Voice;
(3) One Who Has Successfully Followed All the Grand Opera Prima Donnas Who Entered Vaudeville on the Same Bill.

The La Vars, on the other hand, are observed to content themselves with a poetic pronunciamento having a Heine touch, to the effect that " if dancing was coffee with flavor supreme, the Dancing La Vars would furnish the cream "; while Gracie Doyle and Lillianne Rucker, " The Fashion Plates," whisper confidentially that Mrs. Vanderbilt, Mrs. Astor and the other leaders of the Four Hundred deliberately steal from them all their ideas in the way of up-to-date Parisian dress. Mr. Sidney Rosenbaum reveals himself as " The Niftiest Society Comedian

in Vaudeville in his Refined and Ultra Act Entitled
' Spilling the Beans.' "    And one reads with a certain sensation of awe that Miss Estelle de Louvre,
" That Snappy Gal," at present turning 'em away on
the Pantages Circuit, will return to New York in
two months and eat 'em alive with her new classical
Grecian and Athenian dances. . . . The panorama
is one replete with " Smart Entertainers," " International Favorites," " Society's Pets," " Tremendous
Hits," " Classy Dressers " and the like — a veritable field of little violets. . . . Yet a chapter such
as this would be a sorry thing did it neglect to men-
tion one particular, and somewhat larger, violet who
calls himself Stan Stanley.    Mr. Stanley, it appears
from his advertisement, is at once the greatest billiard player in the world, and one whose performances in that line have come as a thunderbolt to all
vaudeville and other art-loving audiences.    Regarding his other philosophies and his attitude toward
the community in general, Mr. Stanley pays for the
necessary space to state :

There are lots of brainless punks who just fiddle their time
away playing pool, while billiard players are all brilliant
men.   It takes your mind off worldly care.   Hoppe made
$80,000 last season.   Did you ever hear of a pool player
making that much?   Learn billiards, boys; it will improve
your act.   Newspapermen and authors play billiards, never
pool.   A billiard player has entrée to the best clubs all over
the country.   A billiard player always mingles with the real
men.   A pool player frequents cellars.   A pool player must
associate with low-brows.   I am only a hardworking comedian, but nevertheless because I can play billiards I go to the
best clubs and meet the finest people all over the country!

Let us now consider for a few brief spaces the " refinement " negotiated by these vaudevillians. The average vaudeville gentleman's idea of getting himself up as a Van Bibber, a clubman, a fashionable, a sort of composite of Ward McAllister, Berry Wall and Freddie Gebhardt, is, first, to put a great quantity of vaseline on his hair and then rub the hair to a high gloss with a bootblack's cloth; second, to employ a large diamond ring upon the index finger of his right hand; and third, to don a top hat a size and a half too large for him. While the average vaudeville lady's idea of inspiring envy in the bosom of Mrs. Vincent Astor is anything pink with a sufficient abundance of silver spangles upon it to make it look like one of the chandeliers in Sherry's. Where, on the so-called legitimate stage, the average young actress' idea of a smart débutante is generally summed up in a bunch of sweet peas and dropping the " H " out of Bar Harbour, the vaudeville young lady's idea would seem for the most part to rest in a pair of pink silk slippers (whatever the colour of the costume), a piece of pale blue tulle in the hair and a line somewhere toward the end of the sketch in which she wistfully confesses that she is tired of the Newport Casino with its airs and affectations and longs once again to have a glass of beer in Stauch's Café down at Coney. The *jeune premier,* or leading juvenile, of the Broadway stage is, as everyone knows, to be distinguished without much difficulty from the wooden furniture and the rest of the actors by virtue of the fact that he always carries a highly polished gold cigarette case and wears a gold key chain draped into his trouser's pocket from the third belt loop. On the Small Time vaudeville stage, the juvenile appearing in a one-act play (or sketch, as it is better known) may be located not quite so readily. Picking out the juvenile here becomes a sort of waiting game. One waits until the most inopportune moment in the dramatic action of the sketch and the young man who then proceeds to do a clog-dance — that young man is the juvenile. It seems to be a tradition of the Small Time vaudeville playlet that whenever a husband comes back from his club unexpectedly and finds his wife in the embrace of her lover, the lover must promptly disengage the wife's arms, emit, for the benefit of the husband, a sarcastic snicker and proceed forthwith to do a bit of a clog, winding up with the conventional pedal *pat-pat* upon the bass drummer's last two bangs.

The twenty trump cards of the Small Time humour, in the order of their respective efficiency, are the following:

1. Cheese [1] (preferably Gorgonzola; second choice, Swiss; third choice, the holes in the Swiss).

[1] *One often wonders at the genesis of the notion that cheese is funny, and that an allusion to it should infallibly cause merriment in a theatre audience. It cannot be because of the perfume of the cheese; for an allusion to the Swiss or the Gorgonzola cheese, which are practically without bouquet, invariably brews a louder laughter than an allusion to such more vehement cheeses as Limburger and Camembert. Nor can it be because the word cheese itself has a comic sound; cheese is a word intrinsically not nearly so funny in sound as, for example, the words chow chow, jelly and cookie, which, though of an exotic Chinese quality, are unavailing for purposes of laughter in the playhouse. Granting that cheese is a ludicrous creature, why should Brie be funny and Liederkranz, which is much like*

2. The dill pickle. (a. The small growths upon the pickle, referred to as "warts." b. The squirting proclivities of the pickle.)
3. Whiskers (preferably their soup-swabbing propensity).
4. Grapefruit (see No. 2, Clause b).
5. The seat of the pants.
6. Monsewer.
7. An onion.
8. Hoboken.
9. Newark.
10. The in-Seine River.
11. A waistcoat of any colour other than black, white, or gray.
12. See No. 5, and attach a piece of fly-paper.
13. The wrist-watch.
14. The Champs Elysées, pronounced the Chumps Lizzie.
15. The remark, "You Big Swede," addressed to a coloured gentleman.
16. An allusion to the wife of the Tsar as the Tsardine.
17. Imprinting a kiss of goodbye on a dollar bill about to be loaned to someone.
18. On making an exit, suddenly bending in at the waist as if expecting a kick from the rear.
19. The remark that Germany is the place where the germs come from.

*it, unfunny? What, in short, makes an audience twit the Swiss, Limburger, Gorgonzola and Roquefort cheeses and be urbane and gracious toward the Edam, Münster, Stilton, Cream, Port-du-Salut and Hand cheeses? That the laughter of an audience is conditioned on the effluvium of the cheese and that it is therefore the effluvium and not the cheese that amuses the audience, one is indisposed to grant. The empyreuma, or sachet, of the finnan haddie, for instance, is of two-fold the eloquence of even the Camembert, yet the audience does not hold jubilee upon a communication regarding the finnan haddie, nor for that matter even the finnan haddie's more vociferous confrère, the smoked herring.*

20. A reference to a washboard as "The Woman's Home Companion."

A careful contemplation of the Small Time vaudevilles brings to light the news that the Small Time vaudevilles would unquestionably have to close up shop were it not for the invention of the word "boob." This word "boob" is to the Small Time vaudevilles what the names Carter, Travers and Jack Grayson have long been to Broadway playwrights and their equivalents in the field of novel writing. From 8:10 P. M., when the curtain lifts on a Small Time vaudeville performance, until 11 P .M., when finally it falls, every act on the bill employs the word at least once and often as many as a dozen times. Every act, that is, except the team of Japanese acrobats — which uses whatever is the Japanese for the word. Precisely what the word "boob" means is a matter to which I am not privy, but one judges from the manner of its employment in the vaudeville halls that the only persons in the world who were not, or are not, "boobs" are General Joffre, Christy Matthewson, President Wilson, Benny Leonard, Teddy Roosevelt, General Pershing and the proprietor of Joel's chile concarne restaurant in West Forty-first Street. The synopsis of four out of every five Small Time sketches, when handed to the performer by the sketch writer commissioned to get up the act, must look much like this:

9:00 P. M.— Curtain.
9:05 P. M.— Someone calls you a boob.

9:10 P. M.— Someone else calls you a big boob.

9:15 P. M.— Someone else calls you a great big boob.

9:20 P. M.— Someone else calls you a great big fat boob.

9:22 P. M.— You turn out to be a very clever detective from Headquarters.

The songs which the artists and artistes of the minor vaudevilles select for rendition may be divided into six classes. These six are:

(1) Songs in which the moon shines down on something.

(2) Songs in which one is assured that one's mother is one's real sweetheart.

(3) Songs in which is emphasized the invincibility of the boys in blue. (No attention is paid to the more recent change to khaki since neither " will be true " nor " to you " can be made to rhyme with it.)

(4) Songs in which are described the amours of an Hawaiian belle and an Irishman named O'Brien.

(5) Songs in which each line of the chorus begins with a certain letter of the alphabet, the letters being grouped together in the last line and spelling some appropriate word.

(6) Songs in which are described the feelings of one person since the other told him that she loved him.

[211]

That the artists and artistes should therefore under the circumstances seek jealously to safeguard their professional position and honour when that position and honour are infringed upon, impeached, or assailed by the less eminent and so envious members of the profession, will be readily understood and appreciated by the mere outsider. And it therefore comes about that in the divers professional gazettes of these artists and artistes one observes a weekly column of repartée replete with vigorous denials and vivid defences, and strewn with piquant and devastating *mots*. From one such journal recently I extracted the appended two instances of righteous indignation. They will serve, I trust, as a sufficiently illuminating picture of the manner in which the artists and artistes conduct their controversies and battle for their firesides and the purity of their professional reputations.

*Exhibit A.*— A letter from Mons. Allaire, of the Three Bounding Allaires, *re* Miss Flo D'Arcy, of The D'Arcy Sisters:

Dear Editor: Please to print this letter as I want to denounce to the world the action of Flo D'Arcy, of The D'Arcy Sisters, who has deliberately pinched my one-armed back spring which was invented solely by me as can be proven by my personal agent Mr. Joe Ludesheimer, who has been my personal agent for years as well as the agent for the Three Bounding Allaires of which I am the personal agent and manager. My one-armed back spring has made a sensation wherever displayed in America or Europe and I want to warn Flo D'Arcy, of The D'Arcy Sisters, that if she

[212]

don't cease it I will prosecute her to the full extent of the law which I have already asked our lawyer, Mr. Isadore P. Klein, to take steps towards.

Thanking you, I am, yours,
AUG. ALLAIRE, of The Three Bounding Allaires.

*Exhibit B.*— A letter from Miss Flo D'Arcy of The D'Arcy Sisters, *re* the above:

Dear Editor: I dislike to be unlady-like, as my conduct as a member of the famous team of D'Arcy Sisters who have played successfully in all parts of the world is well known to all my dear friends in vaudeville always to be strictly ladylike, but I can't let the remarks of one, Aug. Allaire, of The Three Bounding Allaires, go by unnoticed. I want to say to Aug. Allaire that if he claims I stole the one-armed back spring from him he is a liar, as I copied the one-armed back spring from Oscar Delarmo, of Delarmo and Astor, with his kind permission. Mr. Oscar Delarmo has used the one-armed back spring for twenty years and twenty years ago Aug. Allaire of The Three Bounding Allaires, was probably still sweeping out some Baltimore Lunch place on the Bowery.

Faithfully yours,
MISS FLO D'ARCY,
Of the D'Arcy Sisters — booked solid for one year.

What a still fertile field here for the pen of her hat was Helen Green!

# Chapter Sixteen: What Its Public Wants

That it is a most difficult, if not altogether impossible, matter to tell what the public wants is a canard sedulously cultivated and disseminated by those very persons who know exactly what the public wants, who know that giving the public exactly what it wants is as easy as rolling off a cigarette and who, through the crafty promulgation of the canard, contrive shrewdly to have themselves regarded by swallowers of the canard as remarkable and perspicacious creatures possessed of an eerie gift for crystal-gazing, palmistry, tea-leaf-reading, fortune-telling, divination and necromancy in general. Yet the persistence of the delusion that a successful and highly prosperous catering to the public tastes is a rocky road, and one strewn with the corpses of countless adventurers, is indefatigable. Why, it is not easy to say; unless one recalls that such sister delusions as the notion that a cold in the head will if left alone cure itself in nine days and the idea that an expensive cigar is always stronger than a cheap one are equally vigorous and persistent.

The theory that no person knows precisely what it is that the public wants and that the person wh succeeds in giving the public what it wants does so largely as a matter of lucky accident falls to pieces immediately one remembers, first, that the successful person started out with the deliberate idea of giving the public something it wanted and, second, that this same person very often succeeds in giving the public what it wants the next time he tries and the time after that, and the time after that. That this person may in his enterprise fail once in a while does not shatter the statement that the business of giving the public what it wants is more or less a sinecure any more than the failure of a pole vaulter who twice has negotiated some twelve feet two inches and misses the third time shatters the statement that the pole vaulter knows exactly the technique that permitted him to make the previous auspicious attempts. Giving the public what it wants is as simple a matter as elementary mathematics, but it is as unreasonable to suppose, therefore, that the man who understands what the public wants and how to give it to the public must never under any circumstances miss the mark as it would be to suppose, in an equally incomplex direction, that the man who understands how the face must be shaved and how to shave it must therefore never under any circumstances cut himself.

Probably more vehemently than any other class, the persons connected with the theatre proclaim the impossibility of predicting and deciphering the palate of the mob. Yet what are the facts once we inquire into them? In the last decade, how many theatrical managers have failed to make money out of this very same public taste which they allege they are unable accurately to plumb? Klaw and Erlanger, Cohan and Harris, the Shuberts, A. H. Woods, Morosco, Dillingham, Belasco, Comstock, Gest, Ziegfeld, even the young fellows and beginners like Williams, Hopkins, Walker — they've all figured the thing out profitably. And if now and again we find a theatrical manager like the late Charles Frohman who did not so accurately figure out what the public wanted and who therefore did not make so much money, we have the reason not in the fact that it is difficult to figure out what the public wants, but in the fact that, though it is comparatively easy, Mr. Frohman was not entirely privy to the way in which to do it.

Charles Frohman was an impracticable man. He once said, " There is no such thing as ' the ' public. There are a thousand different publics. The manager who talks of ' the ' public is the kind of manager who believes that the public holds meetings in Cooper Union to decide what it likes and doesn't like." And there Mr. Frohman made his mistake and lost money. True, the public does not hold meetings in Cooper Union to settle upon its tastes, but those tastes are every bit as settled upon as if the public did hold meetings in Cooper Union to settle them. Before " Pollyanna " was produced, George Tyler predicted it would make a fortune. Before " Moloch " was produced, George Tyler predicted it would lose money. The only financial failure George M. Cohan has written in the last decade was " The Miracle Man." The night it was produced

[216]

he told me he was extremely dubious that it was what the public wanted. Three days after he read the manuscript of " It Pays to Advertise," and three months before he produced the play, Mr. Cohan told me it was exactly the sort of thing the public wanted and would fill double the purse of Fortunatus. Ziegfeld knows exactly what the public wants, gives it to the public year in and year out in " The Follies "— never failing and playing to as high as $27,000 a week. The Shuberts jam the Winter Garden four times in five. Dillingham crowds the Hippodrome. And Albee packs the Palace with exactly the kind of vaudeville the public wants. The playwrights who sidestep art for art's sake, whose one concern is figuring out the popular taste and coining it into two-dollar bills, make money just as easily. George Cohan has made several fortunes. So has George Broadhurst. George V. Hobart, Goodman, Marcin, A. E. Thomas, Winchell Smith, Megrue, Sheldon — they've all found the thing comparatively easy.

Leaving the theatre for the moment, we find the matter has been quite as absurdly simple for men in other avenues. Robert W. Chambers knows exactly what the public wants and regularly provides the public with what it wants. Irvin Cobb knows almost as well and so does Mary Roberts Rinehart. Richard Harding Davis knew, as Rupert Hughes knows today. To object that this is no fair way to argue, since it is possible these popular writers failed many times before they were able to learn what the public wanted is to interpose an objection that is invalid. Chambers knew from the very beginning — without a single failure! So did Cobb. So did Mary Rinehart. So did the rest. They were successful prognosticators from the start. Their very materially increased rewards today are but the result of their cumulative success in fathoming the popular taste. Cyrus K. Curtis, Harold Bell Wright, Herbert Kaufman, Houdini, three out of every five of the moving picture magnificos, Catherine Chisholm Cushing, Gene Stratton Porter, Gillette the Safety Razor Man, Henry Ford, Elinor Glyn, Bernard Shaw, Eva Tanguay, Theodore Roosevelt, Eleanor Porter and Billy Sunday have figured the thing out in these days just as aptly and as completely as Oscar Hammerstein, Elbert Hubbard, Charles H. Hoyt, Paul Dresser, the Hanlons, Charles Garvice, Albert Ross, P. T. Barnum, Hires of Hires' Root Beer, Charles Klein, Lincoln J. Carter, Imre and Bolossy Kiralfy, Bert Standish, Charles Yale, Lew Wallace, Sir Thomas Lipton, Doctor Beeman and John Philip Sousa figured it out in the yesterdays.

One must grant, obviously enough, that the person planning a financial coup against the popular taste have in hand the fundamental technic of his particular line of activity. For it is unreasonable to demand against the present argument that if the thing is as easy as is here claimed, *anyone* should be able to do it. Each man to his trade. One cannot demand that General Pershing, for example, be able to decipher the public's taste for music shows, or that George Cohan be able to figure out the exact

[218]

way to indent the Hindenburg line. But granted these fundamentals, the matter of giving the mob what it likes becomes a simple business. How many men do you suppose one would encounter in the poor-houses of the United States who had definitely *tried* to give the public what it wanted and had failed? The failures, the paupers, are not those who have tried to sell the public what it wanted but those who have tried to sell to some middleman what they believed the middleman thought the public wanted. . . . The middleman is not in the poor-house.

What does the public want? Leaving for some other statistician the facts that the public wants (with a variation so infinitesimal that it is negligible) *blue* bathing suits, *two* straws with its glass of lemonade and *rectangular* bed pillows, let us confine ourselves here mainly to the case of the theatre. That it is a not especially difficult business to give the public precisely what it wants in the theatre must be immediately apparent to any unprejudiced person who remembers that a theatre audience from time immemorial has never *once* failed to respond at a music show to the device of having the chorus girls throw things — balls, candies, what not — into the auditorium or at a drama to the device of having one character knock a revolver out of the hand of another character or at a vaudeville show to the device of having one comique spray another comique in the face with an atomizer.

There are, in the theatre, approximately one hundred stereotyped and familiar tricks which may be

[219]

relied upon to affect unfailingly a theatre audience — tricks ranging all the way from the elbow that suddenly slips off the edge of a table (a certain laugh-provoker) to the equally positive thrill-brewer of the shattered glass window. The response of a theatrical audience is largely a matter of habit, of tradition, and so the devices which make an audience laugh or weep or experience a tingling of the vertebræ change in the main but little. I, for example, have been going to the theatre professionally — about four nights a week — for the last fourteen years; yet I find that I laugh today at the fat pantaloon who suddenly trips and lands with a loud thud on his *chassis* just the same as I laughed at the same business fourteen years ago. And the much more casual theatregoer, the man who goes to the theatre less frequently, laughs at the thing with a doubled guffaw power. Human nature doesn't change.

Speaking of this and the public's admiration for so-called happy endings to its plays, George Cohan once said to me, " Of course the public likes happy endings in the theatre just as anybody likes happy endings to anything anywhere. It is silly to blame the happy ending taste on a theatrical audience alone. It is as if one were to say, ' When a man gets into a theatre he wants everything to be exactly the opposite of what he wants it to be outside the theatre.' The fact that a man, or woman, pays a couple of dollars to go to a theatre certainly doesn't mean that he or she is paying a couple of dollars to change his or her nature. A man goes to a baseball game to

see the home team win. He goes to a billiard par-
lour to watch a game of billiards between his friend
Bill Botts and another fellow he doesn't like and of
course wants the game to turn out favourably for
friend Bill. He goes to the office in the morning
and, when five o'clock comes, he wants his day to
have turned out a prosperous and a happy day. A
man wants to see those persons he likes or admires
win out. He wants to be happy himself. Wherever he is, whatever he does, whomever he watches!
Why should human nature change — or be expected
to change — the minute it deposits its person in an
orchestra seat? This is why the public wants happy
endings to its plays. Just as a man will overlook
an umpire's somewhat ' off ' decision so long as it
favours his home ball team, so will the public overlook an analogous fault in dramatic logic so long
as it favours its hero and heroine in a play. Show
me a man or woman who down in his heart prefers
an unhappy ending to a play to a happy one and I
will, other things being equal, show you a big
liar. Human nature is the same with all of
us. Some people are just a little more ex-
pert than others in pretending it isn't. But you'll
find that not one of these fibbers or fakers will take
a chance in not picking up a horseshoe, in opening
an umbrella inside the house, in throwing away a
four-leaf clover or in failing to rap on wood and
whistle after he has been boasting that he hasn't
had the old pain in his right leg for the last three
months."

In vaudeville such men as Aaron Hoffman,

Thomas J. Gray and Will Cressy have for years been supplying vaudeville actors with exactly the kind of jokes the vaudeville audiences want. Just as the United Cigar Stores Company figured out that all men like to look at themselves in mirrors and placed large mirrors in each one of their countless stores with eminently satisfactory magnetic results, so has Mr. Gray, for example, figured out that a comic vaudeville monologist who calls the orchestra leader Rudolph will make the vaudeville public laugh itself half to death.

A well-known and experienced publisher has said that one can usually spot a young writer's first attempt at a short fiction story in the fact that it ends with a suicide. And an equally well-known and experienced theatrical producer has said that one can usually spot a young writer's first attempt at playwriting in the fact that the play ends unhappily. From which, since it is pretty generally conceded that the taste of the public in general is to no small degree the taste of its younger element, one might deduce that what the public mostly wanted was sadness. The public does want sadness, but *qualified* sadness. The most profitable theatrical property the world has ever known is the Cinderella story, a tale of pleasurable melancholy. But the most popular attitude toward what we may call " sad " plays is the peculiar one of believing that, since every cloud has a silver lining, the playwright should dramatize the cloud in such a way that the public may see the cloud through the silver lining rather than the silver lining through the cloud. The silver lining, that is, should (technically and figuratively speaking) be placed down-stage (near the footlights) and the cloud up-stage (near the back-drop). The whole business reminds one of the old trick cloudy sentence, " Able was I ere I saw Elba," which reads the same backwards as forwards : it is curious, but it works. . . . To argue that the public does not want sadness in the theatre on the ground that " there's enough trouble in real life without seeing it in the theatre " is to argue that the public does not want happiness in real life because there is enough of it in the theatre.

The Cinderella story, dramatized with the silver lining toward the audience, as playwrights from Carroll Fleming down to Hartley Manners have for the last twenty-five years been proving, is a veritable theatrical mint. It is only when the story is dramatized the other way 'round, as in the case of " Rich Man, Poor Man," that it comes a box-office cropper. And even then a cropper only in part.

Some of the public's invariable preferences are difficult to understand, yet there is no need for the person desiring merely to capitalize such preferences and make money out of them *to* understand them. Such preferences are axioms. Why the public should always want a small button on the top of its cap, or a more or less decorative line of stamped leather two inches this side of the tip of its shoe, or three buttons on the back of the cuff of the sleeve on its sack coat, or black paper with gold letters on its packets of needles, or a little bow in the back of the inside of its derby hat, the oracles would have a difficult time trying to solve. There does not seem to be any good reason for such useless and exotic things; they are, in good truth, just a trifle silly. Yet that is what the public wants — so why not give it to the public? And the same thing holds true in the more relevant case of the theatre and its amusement fare. Your playwright who is in the show business less for the show than for the business knows perfectly well that nine members of the music-show public out of every ten will laugh inordinately at the comedian who, on making his exit, suddenly bends himself in at the bustle as if anticipating a kick from the rear, and at the comedian who, upon being called a Limburger cheese, strikes a heroic attitude like Robert Downing in " The Gladiator " and retorts that those are strong words; so the playwright sticks them off-hand into the libretto in exactly the same way that the cap-maker sticks the little button on top of the cap.

No fair-minded man will believe that a song writer like Irving Berlin or Jerome Kern, for example, just happens accidentally to hit the popular taste almost every time he sits down and writes a new song. The interposing of such an argument is too ridiculous. Such song writers do not merely " hit " the public's taste; they know the public's taste. They know that taste as accurately as the manufacturer of a so-called moving-picture " news weekly " knows a moving-picture theatre audience will inevitably applaud when a regiment of marching soldiers is flashed upon the screen.

There is in New York a large hotel whose man

ager figured out the popular taste accurately and shrewdly enough to appreciate that men in the mass — for all that is claimed to the contrary — like now and then a bit of candy. The hotel man knew that men seldom, if ever, *buy* candy for themselves, so he passed out a few pieces *gratis* to each table in his restaurant, and his restaurant soon began to be talked about. Men liked the place and while, true enough, they did not go around telling about the candy, it was really the candy (as the hotel manager knew) that subconsciously made them talk about the restaurant and go to it equally subconsciously. The restaurant has proved a great success. . . . I myself go there at least once a week.

It is a peculiarity of the world of the theatre that a manager is not regarded as a rich man unless he is a very rich man. To make a mere five hundred or a thousand dollars a week is considered nigh unto failure. And it is doubtless for this reason that the delusion as to the impossibility of deciphering what the public wants exists in the theatre. But it is just that and nothing more — a delusion. The figuring out of what the public wants is an amazingly simple thing.

For instance, one of the things that the public wants is an argument like this.

# Chapter Seventeen: In Conclusion

In the career of the critic of the theatre there are three more or less distinct periods: first, the period in which he passionately believes and vehemently conjures the theatre to be a lyceum of art; second, the period in which he passionately hopes and vehemently prays that the theatre may be a lyceum of art; and third, the period in which he rather good-naturedly comes to the conclusion that his view of the theatre has been all wrong, and doesn't admit it. After fourteen years of professional criticism, I have the honour to announce that I am presently approaching the third period.

That the percussion of wit and idea is considerably less the business of the stage than the percussion of bilbo and rear trouser is an æsthetic to which even the most stubborn-minded critic becomes in time affectingly privy. Yet that he continues thereafter to maintain his old pretence and keep his discovery secret is no more to his discredit than it is to the discredit of a physician to keep the truth from a patient at death's point or to the discredit of a priest to keep confidential a parishioner's confession of sin. For example, the wittiest line of Alfred Capus makes me laugh in the theatre not one-tenth so hard as the spectacle of one pickle-herring clouting another over the ear with a chocolate éclair, but do I admit the fact? I do not. And why? For the same reason that the defending lawyer doesn't admit the avowed guilt of his client. The critic who best serves the theatre must be at once a hypocrite and a surpassing liar. He must stand, a giant and immovable rock, against the tides of truth and honesty. He must, for the good of the theatre, deny with all the vouchers and eloquence at his command that the theatre is a mere place for light amusement, and what is more, he must prove that denial unassailably, incontrovertibly. If the theatre is to be made better, finer, it is to be made so only by a critical conspiracy of silence. The married man lies about the happiness of married life, converts the recalcitrant and doubting bachelor and so serves the race. The historian lies about history, spreads the falsehoods in the school books and so serves his nation by creating in its future peoples a national admiration and a deep patriotism. Parents lie that the virgin and blooming minds of their children may not be sullied by unlovely facts; the church lies that life may be made the more mellow and hope the more reasonable; art itself lies that the truth may be made beautiful. And so, too, the critic of theatrical art must lie. While agreeing that the primary function of the theatre is the stimulation of its audiences' emotions, and that the theatre serves its ends in the degree of such stimuli, he must yet with professorial air pretend to believe that Margaret Mayo's " Baby Mine " is not so laughful as Molière's " Fourberies de Scapin," that Sheldon's " Nigger " is not so thrilling as Maeterlinck's " Death of Tintagiles," that Meyer-Förster's " Old Heidelberg " is not so touching as Ibsen's " Little Eyolf," and that blonde Miss Marion Davies in a blue dress doing nothing, and doing it not particularly well, is not so incendiary as Mrs. Leslie Carter doing "Two Women " with an immense technical fire.

If civilization is the history of repressions, the artistic prosperity of the theatre is the history of critical repressions no less. The idea that the first-rate critic of the theatrical arts who knows Shakespeare's " Merry Wives of Windsor " by heart honestly prefers Shakespeare's " Merry Wives of Windsor " in the theatre to de Caillavet's and de Flers' " The King "— and in the soundest of estimates is more genuinely amused by it — is of a kidney with the idea that he actually finds a greater measure of comical satisfaction in Marcel Vallée's Toby Belch in Copeau's presentation of " Twelfth Night " than in Raymond Hitchcock's photographer in the presentation of " Hitchy-Koo." But to ask the critic frankly to confess to such preferences and frankly to expound their integrity is to ask him to bring the uneducated mob theatregoer down to his own educated theatrical level; in other words, to rend a child's pretty fairy tale, to destroy those illusions of the theatre that, like a desert's blue mirage, lead ever the trusting hopefully on — in short, out of his superior knowledge to rob the theatre of its beautiful faith in Santa Clauses and Little Bright Eyes, in Titanias and Tinker Bells and all the other nixies of an artistic never-never-land. Your astute critic knows better than this. To him, his reader is ever a little Patricia Carleon and he no intruder upon her fond phantasms.

The biography of dramatic criticism is the autobiography of sly hypocrisy. The younger Dumas, a sharp critic, comparing the theatre with the church, said, " You cannot gain the ear of the multitude for any length of time or in any efficacious way save in the name of their higher interests." And then sat himself down and wrote " Camille," which, in the name of the multitude's higher interests, made the multitude slobber over a sentimental prostitute. Hazlitt criticizing ever directly from the intellect, paid his greatest tribute to Joseph Fawcett, a friend who criticized ever directly from the emotions. Where a man who has satirized and made droll mock of his own critical attitude so tidily as Anatole France? And the critic Shaw who wrote that in the theatre he shivered with apprehension as to the potential brutalities of Benedick and Mercutio whenever they approached a woman or an old man is the same playwright Shaw who wrote Bill Walker, Edstaston and a round dozen like them.

It always has been that the critic has eloquently professed one thing about the theatre while he was a critic and has then promptly pulled off his slouch hat and whiskers when he turned playwright and done exactly the opposite. The dramatic criticisms of Robert de Flers in " Figaro " and his subsequent comic opera " Les Travaux d'Hercule " and comedy " Les Sentiers de la Vertu " are as hard to reconcile one with the other as are the criticisms of Jules Lemaitre in the " Journal des Débates " and his

subsequent " Révoltée." To read Wedekind's " Art
of the Theatre " and other critical papers and then
see his plays is to smile broadly into one's cuff. To
read Bahr, the critic, in the Vienna *Tageblatt*, and
then to lay an eye to Bahr, the playwright, in " The
Mother " or " The Apostle " is to negotiate a hollow cough. The Charles Lamb of criticism is hardly
the Charles Lamb of the prevenient farce " Mr. H."
Victor Hugo, the critic of " Le Conservateur Littéraire," is a twenty-eighth cousin to Victor Hugo,
the dramatist of " Le Roi S'Amuse." . . . And
seizing the parachute and dropping a thousand miles,
we behold Mr. Clayton Hamilton, to whom little
appears critically palatable save Molière and Shakespeare, writing " The Big Idea " for production by
George Cohan, and, what is even more droll, Mr.
George Jean Nathan, to whom little appears critically palatable save French farce and Ziegfeld, writing the Scandinavian " Eternal Mystery." What
an obscene clowning is indeed on the world!

But as man's conscious self-deception as to woman's superior spirituality is vital to the prosperity of
society, so this conscious critical gullery is essential
to the highest interests of the theatre. No first-
rate, or even second-rate, critic any longer believes
that the stage is the place for thought, or views the
theatre as an educational institution. The nearest
the stage ever gets to thought is the presentation and
re-establishment of an accepted platitude in terms
of an unaccepted ratiocination. Thus, such a so-
called thoughtful play as " Man and Superman " is
simply the accepted Schopenhauer platitude or

[230]

woman the pursuer expounded in what to a theatre
audience that has always accepted the platitude with
a deadly seriousness, has hitherto been to that audience an unaccepted sportive dialectic. Thus, again,
such a so-called thoughtful play as Bergstrom's
" Karen Borneman " is merely the accepted de Lam-
bert platitude on the command of the passions expounded in what to a theatre audience that since the
time of Congreve has accepted the platitude with
a light heart, has hitherto been to that audience an
unaccepted tragic dialectic.

Secondly, no first-rate, or even second-rate, critic
longer believes that the stage is the place for fine
dramatic literature since, save on very rare occasions, the presentation of fine dramatic literature is
left entirely in the hands of amateurs, and since amateurs, for all their initial acumen, are scarcely happy
in bringing to fine dramatic literature the histrionic
experience, the finish and warmth, essential to its
prosperous interpretation. To object here that this
is a very silly argument since it offers no reason why
fine dramatic literature should not therefore all the
more find its place upon the professional stage is to
believe that the professional actor who enjoys all
the experience, finish and warmth that the amateur
lacks, enjoys at the same time the amateur's intelligence. Can you, in all the theatres of the world,
and more particularly in the English-speaking theatres, think of a carefully deduced company of professional actors able to interpret for instance, Dunsany's " Gods of the Mountain " half way to your
satisfaction? Can you, in all the theatres of the

world, think of a single stage producer able to produce, to the full of your imagination, the " Dream
Play " of Strindberg? Fine dramatic literature, in
short, belongs not upon the stage, but in the library.
The theory, revered in certain quarters, that all plays
are written to be acted or they are not plays is of a
piece with the theory that all music is written to be
sung or it is not music. Some plays are too beautiful for the spoken stage; they are orchestrated alone
for the strings of the silent imagination. . . . A
poem need not be recited aloud to be a poem.

In a word, the discerning critic comes to realize
that the place of the theatre in the community is
infinitely less the place of the university, the studio
and the art gallery than the place of the circus, the
rathskeller and the harem. The theatre is no more
to be appraised from the point of view of the casual
college doctor who once in a while finds his alien way
into it than the bar-room is to be appraised from the
point of view of the prohibitionist. The theatre is,
simply, plainly — and in the soundest critical defi-
nition — a place where a well-educated, well-bred,
well-fed man may find something to divert him pleas-
antly for a couple of hours. And how is this well-
educated, well-bred, well-fed man to be diverted?
Certainly not by so-called intellectual drama, for if
he desired intellectual stimulation he would go to a
lecture chamber or a comradely ale clinic or stay at
home and read. Certainly not by an ostentatious
spectacle of good manners, for good manners are
no novelty to him and did he crave an immediate
pageant of them all he would need do is call upon

one of his friends. Certainly not by fine literature, for fine literature is less a diversion to him than a regular habit. And certainly not by any analogous thing that is part and parcel of his routine. What he wants is the opposite of that to which he is accustomed. In brief, diversion by contrast, by æsthetic shock. And this is what he looks to the theatre to provide him. He wants horse-play, belly laughter, pretty girls, ingenious scenery, imported ladies of joy and eminent home talent, insane melodrama, lovely limbs, lively tunes, gaudy colours, loud humours, farce, flippancy, fol-de-rol. He wants Billy B. Van above Robert B. Mantell, Ann Pennington above Olga Nethersole, the " Follies " above " The Wild Duck," Urban at his worst above Copeau at his best, the slapstick above the sceptre of Claudius — life, colour, movement and gaiety above problems, monotones, technique and authentic merit.

This, then, is the fairest critical view of the theatre. But since it is obviously directed at and from only the best type of theatregoer it is, in like obviousness, not safely to be divulged to the masses. Of this the sincere critic is ever deeply appreciative. He realizes that the average theatregoer is under-educated and under-bred and thus not æsthetically ready for the custard pie arts which are meet for his well-educated and well-bred brother. A boy's constitution must be fortified with pure milk before he may, as a man, amuse himself with ethyl alcohol; a boy must know the Bible before Rabelais, ladies before geishas, addition before subtraction. And, in like manner, the average illiterate theatregoer must be confronted steadily with pure artistic thoughts and elevated purposes and his footsteps set with diligence and care in the direction of the so-called literary drama and the drama of ideas that he may in time gain the necessary background we all of us must gain ere we are privileged to cavort before it. And so, gentlemen, when I write in the public prints that I enjoy the comedy of Shakespeare more than the comedy of Harry Watson, Jr., I lie. Just as I lie when with all my familiar and persuasive eloquence I prove that I find a greater theatrical pleasure in Tolstoi than in the dancing of Doloretes. My only apology is that I lie, and nobly, for the good of the theatre.

* * *

These superficially unseemly thoughts obtrude as I consider the case such a play as Mr. Jesse Lynch Williams' "Why Marry?" When, several years ago, I read Mr. Williams' play — it was known originally by the title "And So They Were Married"— I enjoyed it immensely. It impressed me as a well-written, amiably sophisticated and unusually witty little piece of work. But when, several months ago, I saw Mr. Williams' well-written, amiably sophisticated and unusually witty play in the theatre, I quite frankly confess to having had a poor evening of it. The reasons are not complex. In the first place, where it took me a little less than an hour to read the little play in the warm comfort of my rooms, it took me exactly two hours and a half to engage it in a draughty theatre. Where its pleasant light humours were ample to divert me and win me completely in a leisure library hour, these same pleasant light humours were altogether too meagre to cover an inflated two and one-half hours of stage traffic in which the amiable little play I had so enjoyed in the reading was with the conventional rudeness subjected to actors who absurdly delayed their several entrances that they might, in the Broadway vernacular, " get a hand," to the stereotyped actor pauses after good lines by way of forcing the audience's laughter, to the elaborate emphasizing of points and hocus-pocus of " dressing " the stage and crossings and sittings and emotional byplays and battles for the centre of the stage and takings of bows at the ends of the acts and irrelevant curtain speeches and all the like theatrical rigmarole.

To withstand the effects of such stage devastations, Mr. Williams' intrinsically meritorious play is, for me, of too tender a theatrical skin. It lacks as a show all that it possesses as a play. Compared promiscuously and not a little drolly in local quarters with the work of Shaw, it is deficient in all those show qualities which the latter dramatist, having once been a critic, realizes are essential to the protection and salvation of wit upon the acted stage. After a turn at wits, you will always find the wily Celt bolstering up things for his literate audiences — and his illiterate actors — with a turn at slapsticks. In this wise, he at once preserves his text from stupid mummers and for intelligent auditors. Thus, his Patiomkin of " Great Catherine," after each witty observation, invariably wipes his nose with his dressing gown or falls peremptorily upon his hindquarters or issues an amazing expectoration or kicks the person addressed in the hip-pocket. Thus, in like situation, his Cleopatra jabs Cæsar with a pin and paddles the rear Ftatateeta with a snake-skin, his Inca makes his moustachios jump up and down by pulling a hidden string, his Tanner grabs a chauffeur by the legs and makes him waddle like a wheel-barrow, his Bentley Summerhays throws a fit on the carpet. . . . Mr. Williams, a theatrical idealist, on the other hand sets his wit upon the cold stage nude and shivering, and leaves it there crying for a clothing of extrinsic theatrical stratagems, crying to be taken back home to the library. And so I repeat that such a play as Mr. Williams' is a play of a quality decidedly and unmistakably superior to the plays we commonly get on our native popular stage and, by the same mark and accordingly, a play not so appropriate to a stage designed for purposes of diversion as the decidedly and unmistakably inferior, but vastly more gay and sprightly, play of the basically not dissimilar type of Miss Clare Kummer's " Successful Calamity."

### THE END